HISTORY OF THE COINAGE OF THE TERRITORIES OF THE EAST INDIA COMPANY IN THE INDIAN PENINSULA

HISTORY OF THE COINAGE OF THE TERRITORIES OF THE EAST INDIACOMPANY IN THE INDIAN PENINSULA

AND

CATALOGUE OF THE COINS IN THE MADRAS MUSEUM.

WITH TWENTY PLATES.

BY

EDGAR THURSTON

SUPERINTENDENT, GOVERNMENT CENTRAL MUSEUM,
MADRAS,

GYAN

Published by

Gyan Publishing House
5, Ansari Road
Daryaganj, New Delhi-110002
Phone: 011-47034999, 9811692060
E-mail: books@gyanbooks.com

Distribution Network
gyanbooks.com
India, USA, Canada, UK, Australia, France

ISBN : 978-81-212-3539-6 (PB)
First Published, 1890

2nd Impression 2020

Printed at: Gyan Press, Delhi.

History of the Coinage of the Territories of the East India Company in the Indian Peninsula
Author: Edgar Thurston

GOVERNMENT CENTRAL MUSEUM,
MADRAS.

HISTORY OF THE COINAGE OF THE TERRITORIES OF THE EAST INDIA COMPANY IN THE INDIAN PENINSULA:

AND

CATALOGUE OF THE COINS IN THE MADRAS MUSEUM.

With Twenty Plates.

BY

EDGAR THURSTON,

SUPERINTENDENT, GOVERNMENT CENTRAL MUSEUM, MADRAS.

MADRAS:
PRINTED BY THE SUPERINTENDENT, GOVERNMENT PRESS.

1890.

PREFACE.

In the preparation of the present work, which gives a general sketch of the early development of the East India Company and of its coinage, to which I have added a catalogue of those coins which are contained in the collection of the Madras Museum, I have received great assistance from Bruce's "Annals of the Honorable East India Company," Neumann's "Beschreibung der bekanntester kupfermünzen," and Weyl's "Verzeichniss von Münzen und Denkmünzen der Jules Fonrobertschen sammlung."

To the British Museum I am greatly indebted for casts of many coins which are not in the Madras Museum collection.

When recently in Europe I was able to procure from the coin-dealers many coins which are either rare, or, so far as I know, not to be obtained at all, in India at the present day. I then, too, became aware, for the first time, that Atkins' "Coins and Tokens of the Possessions and Colonies of the British Empire" was in the press, and to this book, which has since been issued, I acknowledge my indebtedness.

No attempt has been made by me to give a complete record of the various proof and pattern pieces, though some are referred to and described.

In 1887 I was engaged in going carefully over the records of the Madras Mint, from which such information was extracted as I thought to be of value and interest. The opportunity of examining, in like manner, the records of the other Indian mints did not offer itself; but it is to be hoped that this somewhat ungrateful task will eventually be carried out by numismatists in the other Presidencies.

The plates were lithographed by Kell and Son from drawings made by a Native draftsman. The coins figured on plates i to xvi are in the Madras Museum collection, which is wanting in those figured on plates xvii to xx.

EDGAR THURSTON.

January 1890.

I.—HISTORY OF THE COINAGE.

HISTORY OF THE COINAGE OF THE TERRITORIES OF THE EAST INDIA COMPANY IN THE INDIAN PENINSULA:

AND

CATALOGUE OF THE COINS IN THE MADRAS MUSEUM.

In the year 1599 an Association of Merchant Adventurers was 1599.
formed to embark what Bruce says,[1] "was then considered a large stock on a voyage to the East Indies. The contract of these adventurers is valuable, from its being the first authentic deed which occurs in the annals of an East India trade; it is entitled 'The names of suche p'sons as have written with their owne handes, to venter in the p'tended voiage to the Easte-Indias (the which it maie please the Lorde to prosper) and the somes that they will adventure; the xxij September 1599.' The fund subscribed amounted to £30,133 6*s.* 8*d.*, which was divided into one hundred and one shares or adventures, the subscriptions of individuals varying from £100 to £3,000."

At "an assemblie of the committies or y$_{e}$ direct$_{ors}$ of the viage the xxvth of Septemb$_{r}$ 1599" it was resolved that a petition shal be exhibited to y$_{e}$ LL. of her ma$_{es}$ most honorable privy counsell in the name of the adventuro$_{r}$ shewing ther honors that divers merchaunts induced by the successe of the viage pformed by the Duche nation [who] and beinge informed that the duchemen prepare for a newe viage and to that ende have bought divers ships heere in England, were stirred vp w$_{th}$ noe lesse affection to advaunce the trade of ther native cuntrey then the duche merchaunts were to benefite ther comon wealthe, and vppon that affection have resolved to make a viage to the Est Indias yf her ma$_{ie}$ wil be pleased to add to ther entention the better to pforme the enterprise, these severall petitions or Requests following, viz.:—

"To graunt to the adventures a priviledge in succession and to incorporate them in a companie for that the trade of the Indias being so farre remote from hence cannot be traded but in a joint and a vynted stock.

"That the shipping of the adventuro$_{rs}$ being prepared for ther viages be not staied vppon anie pretence of [anie] service for y$_{t}$ the stay of one moneth loseth the oportunetie of a whole yeres viage.

---

[1] *Annals of the Honorable East India Company from* 1600–1707-8, by John Bruce, Esq., M.P., F.R.S., Keeper of His Majesty's State Papers, and Histiographer to the Honorable East India Company. London, 1810; vol. i, p. 111.

"That it may be lawfull for the adventurors anie Stat notwth-standing to sende out forrein coyne, and yf ther shal be a want of forrein coyne to furnishe this present viage that ther may be quyned in her maee mynt so muche forrein quyne as shal be brought in by the adventurors or by ther meanes."

1600-1. On the last day of the year 1600, being the 43rd year of the reign of Queen Elizabeth, the first Royal Charter was issued for erecting an East India Company. By this Charter the Queen (upon the Petition of the Earl of Cumberland, and Two hundred and fifteen other Persons, among whom were several Knights and Aldermen of London, praying the Queen's licence to adventure and set forth one or more Voyages, by way of Traffic and Merchandise, to the East Indies, in the Countries and Parts of Asia and Africa, and to the islands thereabouts; divers of which Countries and Islands had been long since discovered, though not frequented in Trade and Merchandise) incorporated the said Earl and other persons, by the name of "The Governor and Company of Merchants of London trading into the East Indies."

On the 8th of October 1600, the following ships were taken up for the first voyage, and assigned over to five of the Committee of seventeen Directors, to whom the management of the business was entrusted, in trust for the Adventurers :—

	Men.	Tons.
The Malice Scourge	200	600
The Hector	100	300
The Ascension	80	260
The Susan	80	240
A pinnace	40	100

At a General Meeting of the Adventurers held in the same month (October 1600) it was resolved that the management of the concern should be conducted, in future, by twenty-four Committees or Directors, instead of seventeen. These twenty-four Directors were elected on the 30th October 1600, and Alderman Thomas Smith was chosen the first Governor.

The arrangements for the first voyage being nearly complete, the Society of Adventurers resolved "that the goodes shipped by the Companie, and the caskes, shall be marked with this genrall marke, as in the mergent, and that an iron be prepared, whch shall make the saide marke." This trade mark was subsequently reproduced on the copper coinage of the Company.

Concerning the earliest coinage of the Company Ruding says: [1] "By virtue of a Commission, dated January 11 in the same year (1600 or 1601), money was made of a kind unknown to the British mint either before or since her (Elizabeth's) time, for it was by law exportable, and intended for the use of the East India Company. It bore on one side the Queen's Arms, and on the other a portcullis; and was called either India money, from the purpose for which it was struck, or portcullis money, from the device impressed upon it. The weight of it was regulated according to the respective weights of the Spanish piastre, or piece of eight reas, and the half, the quarter, and half-quarter of the same (pl. xvii,

[1] *Annals of the Coinage of Great Britain and its Dependencies.* Third ed., 1840, vol. i, p. 353.

1–4), though they are now usually called the crown, half-crown, shilling, and sixpence. Some coinage of this sort was necessary, for the Queen, when she first incorporated the East India Company, would not permit them to transport the King of Spain's silver coins to the East Indies, though she was frequently solicited by the merchants. The reason which they assigned to induce her to grant this permission determined her to strike coins for the particular purpose of circulation in Asia. They represented to her Majesty that her silver coin and stamp were not known in the East Indies, which they supposed would induce her to grant them a licence to send thither what silver they pleased. The Queen and her Privy Council replied that, for the very reason alleged, it was her fixed and unalterable resolution not to permit them to send the coin of the King of Spain, or of any foreign prince, to India; and that no silver should be exported by her merchants but only such as should be coined with her effigies and picture on the one side, and the portcullis on the other, of the just weight and fineness of the Spanish pieces of eight and pieces of four rials.[1]

"Her prudent reason for this was that her name and effigies might hereafter be respected by the Asiatics, and she be known as great a prince as the King of Spain.

"Of this money, however, they were not to be permitted to export what quantity they thought fit, but only so much as the Queen and her Privy Council should approve of; for her Majesty declared that she held it as a special and chief prerogative of her crown and dignity to put the portcullis upon all the silver the Company should send to the East Indies; and that she would have her merchants, as to the quantity to be exported, subordinate to her will, and not her will to be ruled at the merchants' pleasure."[2]

The Crown or Piece of Eight Reals (pl. xvii, 1) bears on the obverse the English shield crowned in the centre, with the initials E.R. crowned at the sides, and the legend O : ELIZABETH : D : G : ANG : FRA : ET : HIB : REGINA; on the reverse a portcullis crowned, and the legend O : POSVI : DEVM : ADIVTOREM : MEVM. with chains. The Half Crown or Piece of Four Reals (pl. xvii, 2) and Shilling or Piece of Two Reals (pl. xvii, 3) are similar to the crown, except that they have HIBER : on the obverse; while the

---

[1] Notwithstanding this determination the pieces have her arms and not her portrait on the obverse.

[2] "*Violet's Appeal to Cæsar*, page 25, where he has given the figure of the piece of the eight reas, which he calls the true figure of the silver coin that Queen Elizabeth allowed the East India merchants to send to those Indies. He has also given the representation of three square weights (marked respectively India VIII testernes, India IIII testernes, and India II), as being the standard poises of the abovesaid coin remaining in his Majesty's mint, within the Tower of London, and in the custody of Sir William Parkhurst, Warden of his Majesty's said mint. See also *Folkes*, p. 61, and *Leake*, p. 255. Malynes says, that of these pieces were coined in the Tower of London for a trial (in January 1600) some six thousand pounds, which could not be made current in the East Indies, because the Spanish pieces of eight royals had been before that time counterfeited by other nations, which made the East Indians to doubt of our coin, although without cause. [*Lex Mercatoria*, pt. 1, chap. 35, p. 135]" Ruding, op. cit., p. 354, foot-note.

sixpence or Real (pl. xvii, 4) is similar to the half-crown and shilling, except that the legend on the obverse ends with REGIN or REGI.

1602. The first expedition of the Adventurers reached Acheen on the 5th of June 1602, and returned to the Downs on the 11th of September 1603, having on the homeward voyage taken in cargo at Bantam in the Island of Java, where the privileges of trade were acquired from the king, and a factory or house of trade was started.

1604. The following is a copy of a Commission of James I, dated 23rd of February 1604, authorising the East India Company to export the value of £12,000 in foreign coin:—

"James by the grace of God, etc. To all men to whom theise p'esentes shall come greetynge. Whereas our late deare sister Elizabeth by her l'res patents under the greate seale of England bearing date at Westm' the one and thirtith day of December in the three and fortith year of her raigne did uppon peticion made unto her by her deare and lovinge cosen George earle of Cumb'-land and divers other her welbeloved subjects for her royall assent and licence to be graunted unto them that they at their owne adventure costs and charges as well for the honor of this realme of England as for the increase of navigation and advancement of trade of merchandise within the same mighte adventure and sett fourthe certayne voyages with a convenient nomber of shippes and pynnaces by waie of traffique and merchandize into the East Indies in the countries and parts of Asia and Africa did incorporate the saide petitioners into a bodie politique by the name of the governour and companie of the marchaunts of London tradinge into the East Indies to have houlde and enjoy the sole benefit of the trade and trafficque of the saide Easte Indies for the space of fifteene years from the birth of our Lord God then last paste before the date of the said l'res patents. And whereas by the saide l'res patents licence is graunted to the saide governour and companie of marchaunts of London tradinge into the East Indies to t'ansporte oute of this realme into the saide Indies in everie of their voyages duringe saide tearme of fifteene yeares all such forrein coyne of silver Spanishe or other forreyn silver or bullion of silver as they shall duringe the saide tearme bringe or cause to be broughte into this realme of England from the parts beyond the seas either in the same kynde sorte stampe or fashion which it shall have when they bryngе it in or anie other forme stampe or fashion to be coyned in the mynte within the Tower of London soe as the whole quantyties of coyne or monies by them to be transported in anie their saide voyages duringe the saide terme doe not exceede the value of thirtie thousande pounds in any one voiage and so as the som'e of six thousand poundes at the leaste parcell of the same som'e or value of thirtie thousande poundes soe to bee transported as aforesaide be first coyned within the saide Tower of London before the same shal bee transported in anie the saide voyages as by the saide l'res patents more at large appeareth. Nowe forasmuch as the saide governour and company of the saide marchants since the saide l'res patents to them granted have made one voyage in the saide East Indies and retourned their shippes from thence laden with sondry kinds of marchandize and have alsoe prepared and are readie to set forth another voiage into the saide East Indies and they the saide governor and company being desirous and endevouring by all good meanes to manage and carry their saide trade as neere as they can rather by the t'ansportac'on of the native com'odities of our kingdomes and by the bartering and exchange of them for forren com'odities then by using the benefit granted them by the said l'res patents for the carying out of so much tresure in every of their voiages doe content themselves in this p'esent voyage with the lib'ty of t'ansportac'on of twelve thousand pounds in forrein coyne without t'ansportac'on of anie other coyne bulloyn or silver and to that end have made humble peticyon unto us that they may t'ansport the saide value of twelve thousand pounds of forreyn coine without coyning the same or anie part thereof in our mynt within our Tower of London the rather for that they found by experience in their last voiage that they could not without great difficulty and some losse to the said marchants in the value of their monies newe coyned for that voiage make trade for their marchandize in the said East Indies because the said mony being stamped with the ymage and sup'sricpc'on of our said deare sister was strange and unknowne to the people of those parts and the monies now to [be] coyned in our said mint being to be coined with a new stamp of our owne ymage and sup'scripc'on will nott only draw them into the like hindrance in their trade when they shall come into the saide Indies but will cause their shipps which are nowe allmoste ready to depart in their voiage to stay and to be detained here to their further damage and hindrance untill new stamps for the coyning of the said monies in our mynt shall be graven and made for that purpose. Wee therefore favouring the saide marchants and being desirous to give them all furtherance and expedic'on in their p'esent intended voiage of our esp'iall grace ce'ten knowledge and mere moc'on have granted and by theis p'esents for our heires and successors doe grant unto the said governor and company of marchants tradyng into the East Indies that it shall and may bee lawfull for them their factors and assignes in thys p'esent intended voiage which is prepared or in p'eparing for the second voiage into the said East Indies to t'ansport out of this our realme of England all such forreyn coyne or silver either Spanish or other forrein silver as they have prepared p'cured or gotten or shall prepare p'cr'se or gett being already broughte or to be broughte from the parts beyond the seas before the dep'ting of their shipps out of the river of Thames so as the wholl quantity of the coyne and monies by them to be t'ansported in this their p'esent intended voiage being the second voiage toward the said Indies does not exceed the saide value of twelve thousand pounds the same to be t'ansported in the same kinde sort stamp or fashion as the said moneys is or shal be p'cured gotten or broughte into this realme of England and that withoute anie newe coyning or alte'ing of the said monies or anie part thereof from the stampe which it beareth. Anie statute restraint p'hibic'on in that behalf to the cont'ary in any wise notwithstanding. In witness whereof, etc. Witness ourself at Westim' the xxiijth day of February."

B

A quarter Real of James I, bearing on the obverse a thistle and portcullis with chains, and on the reverse an anchor-cross, is referred by Weyl to the Madras Presidency.[1]

1612. In 1612 trade was opened with Surat by Mr. Kerridge, who was well received by the merchants and inhabitants, but opposed by the Portuguese. The Company's ships were attacked by the Portuguese at Swally on the 29th of November 1612, and repulsed. In the following month a Firman was obtained from the Emperor of Delhi, allowing the English to establish a factory at Surat, where Captain Best left ten persons with a stock of £4,000 to purchase goods or provide an investment for him. The agreement with the Governor of Surat for allowing to the English liberty of trade at that port, in addition to other stipulations, contained one to the effect that the English should be allowed to settle factories at the cities of Amadevar (Ahmedhabad), Cambaya, and Goga, as well as at Surat.

1614. On the 14th of January 1614, in compliance with the wishes of the Company, King James I granted a commission to Sir Thomas Roe "to be Ambassador to the Great Mogul, or King of India." The Governor of Surat was dismissed, and a treaty concluded with the Mogul, in which it was stipulated, *inter alia*, that the English should have liberty of trade, and be allowed to settle factories in any port of the Mogul empire, specifying Bengal, Scindy, and Surat.

1615. Meanwhile the Company was making considerable progress with its commercial speculations on the Malabar coast, and Captain Keelinge, on his arrival at Cranganore in March 1615, obtained liberty of trade and permission to settle a factory; and it was agreed by treaty that the English and the Zamorin should join their forces, and expel the Portuguese from Cochin, which, when conquered, should be ceded to the English, they paying one half of the expenses of the expedition, and the Zamorin the other half.

1616. In the following year (1616) a Dutch ship was wrecked near Surat, and ten merchants were left there as the managers of a projected trade, the remainder of the officers and crew proceeding overland to the factory at Masulipatam.[2]

1625. In 1625 the English President and Council at Batavia submitted to the Court to direct their attention to the trade on the Coromandel coast, and dispatched a vessel to Masulipatam. Further, having obtained from the Naig, or Chief of the district, a piece of ground, the English erected a factory at Armagon, which it was intended to make a subordinate agency to Masulipatam.

1628. On account of the oppressions which the English factors at Masulipatam experienced at the hands of the native Governor of that port, it was resolved in 1628 to abandon the factory at that

---

[1] Cuartino (¼ Real, o.J.) Distelkopf, Fallgilter, an den Seiten mit Ketten versehen. *Rf.* Ankerkreutz mit ·.· in den Winkeln. Weyl.

[2] Note from "Hobson-Jobson" by Colonel Henry Yule and Arthur Coke Burnell, 1886. "1789. Masulipatam, which last word, by the way, ought to be written, Machlipatan (Fish-town) because of a whale that happened to be stranded there 150 years ago." Note on *Seir Mutagherin*, iii, 370.

place, leaving behind only one of the factors to recover the debts. The representation of the Agents at Bantam to the President and Council at Surat of the necessity of being supplied with Coromandel cloths, to furnish that station and the Southern markets with the means of increasing their investments in pepper and spices, had determined the Presidency to re-establish the factory at Masulipatam, and to strengthen Armagon; and the necessary 1632.
authority to do so was obtained in November 1632.

A Firman was obtained on the 2nd of February 1633 for 1633.
liberty of trade to the English in the Province of Bengal, without any other restriction, than that the English ships were to resort only to the port of Pipley. This event marks the date at which the English first obtained the right to enter the Ganges, and those countries which, subsequently, opened up a most lucrative trade.

In 1639 Mr. Day, one of the Council at Masulipatam, was sent 1639.
to explore the country in the neighbourhood of the Portuguese station at St. Thomé, and reported that Madraspatan[1] was a situation, at which, in his opinion, the best coast goods could be procured. The land was purchased from the Raja of Chandragiri and, without waiting for orders from the Court, Mr. Day commenced building, at the expense of the Company, a fortification to which the name of Fort St. George was given. The continuation of this work was ordered later by the President and Council of Surat, and the new station, to which the factory of Masulipatam was transferred, made subordinate to Bantam.

The early gold coin of Madras was the *pagoda*, a word which, Moor says[2] "is a word altogether unknown beyond the corrupting influence of European colloquial example, whether used descriptively of a coin or a temple; the former being generally called by Hindus *Pun*.

"As to the word pagoda, applied either to a coin or a temple, to the latter especially it ought to be dropped as inaccurate and barbarous, and not at all used by the natives out of the reach of European tradition. I find an attempt to derive the word from *Mahomedan* authority, imagining that anti-idolatrous people to have called the temples of the *Hindus* by the debasing but accurate appellation of *bút-gáda*: from *bút*, an idol, and *gáda*, a temple. Bartholomeo says the coin, being impressed with the goddess Bhagavada, is, therefore, so called: pagoda being a corruption or abbreviation. But, admitting Bhagavada to be a name of Dévi, and to be borne by some *puns*, it would apply to such only; whereas we give it to all gold coins of about the value of seven or eight shillings, be the impression what it may. And, indeed, I have lately seen a silver coin, worth about four shillings, with the word *pagoda*, or half *pagoda*, in English, with

---

[1] Note from Yule and Burnell, op. cit. "1672...... following upon Madraspatan, otherwise called *Chinnepatan*, where the English have a fort called St. George, chiefly garrisoned by *Toepasses* and *Mistices*; from this place they annually send forth their ships, as also from Suratte." *Baldœus*, Germ. ed., 152.

1726. "The Town or Place, anciently called *Chinapatnam*, now called Madraspatnam and Fort St. George." *Letters Patent*, in *Charters of East India Company*, 368-9.

[2] Hindu Pantheon. Ed. 1864, pp. 310-11.

some oriental characters stamped on it, and a representation of a Hindu temple. This coin I imagine to be intended for Madras, and cannot but lament that so miserable a specimen of our taste and talents should be suffered to go forth. To say that the execution is worthy of the design is to stigmatise both with deserved reprobation." Writing about the Pagoda, Dr. Bidie remarks[1] "The common Tamil name for the pagoda is Varáha, an appellation due to the circumstance that some of the older types had on the obverse the figure of a *Varáha* or *Boar*, the symbol of the Chalukyas and kings of Vijayanagar, or the image of Vishnu in the Varáha *avatár*. The Hindustani name of the pagoda is *Hun*, a word probably derived from *Honnu*, the Canarese designation of the half pagoda. That the Mahomedans should have adopted this corruption of the Canarese term for the coin is explained by the fact that, when they invaded the Carnatic, they first saw the pagoda or half pagoda in the hands of a Canarese-speaking people. According to Sir Walter Elliot the term *varáha* is never used in ancient Tamil records in connection with money, but the word *pon*, which was a piece equal to the modern half pagoda, the pagoda itself being the double *pon*, which ultimately became the *varáha*."

Speaking of the Chandragiri Pagoda Marsden says:[2] "*Chandragiri* or Chandergherry, which gives name to these huns, is a town in the Karnatik, formerly the capital of what was called by our early travellers the kingdom of *Narsingha*, in consequence of its having been rendered a place of great strength by *Narsingha Rájá* of *Vijayanagara*. After the conquest of the latter city by the Mahometan States of the peninsula, in the sixteenth century, a descendent of *Narsingha* transferred the seat of Hindu government to *Chandra-giri*, from whence the last of the race was expelled in 1646. It was from one of these rájás that the English East India Company purchased, in the year 1620, the spot of ground on which stood the old fort and factory of Madras, now inclosed within the works of Fort St. George, together with the privilege of coining money, under the stipulation that the English should not fail to preserve on their coinage the representation of that deity, who was the favourite object of his worship. . . . . . The female figure on the obverse appears to be that of *Lakshmi*. There are other specimens precisely resembling this as to the reverse, which have three erect figures (a male accompanied by two females) on the obverse, whose costume denotes them to be mortal rather than divine personages. These are vulgarly termed three-*swámi*[3] pagodas, and

[1] Journ. As. Soc., Beng., 1888, p. 35.

[2] Numismata Orientalia, 1826, pt. ii, p. 739, pl. xlviii, fig. mlxxvi.

[3] Notes from Yule and Burnell, op. cit.

"Swamy, Sammy, s. This word is a corruption of the Skt. swâmin, 'Lord.' It is especially used in South India, and in two senses: (a) a Hindu idol; especially as Sammy, in the dialect of the British soldier. This comes from the usual Tamil pronunciation sâmi; (b) the Skt. word is used by Hindus as a term of respectful address.

"Swamy-pagoda, s. A coin formerly current at Madras; probably so called from the figure of an idol on it. Milburn gives Swamy-pagodas = 110 Star Pagodas. A '*three*-swâmi pagoda' was a name given to a gold coin bearing on the obverse the effigy of Chenna Keswam Swâmi (a title of Krishna) and on the reverse Lakshmi and Rukmini."

weigh 2 dwt. $4\frac{1}{2}$ grs. M. Tavernier's Plate Nos. 5 and 6 are imperfect representations of them under the name of the rájá of Carnatica's pagoda." According to Dr. Bidie[1] the standing figures on this pagoda are intended to represent Venkatesvara and his two wives. In connection with this coin Sir Walter Elliot writes[2]:—"The type of the first class (having the standing figure of Vishnu, with or without his two wives, on the obverse, and a granulated reverse) appears to have been derived from the favour in which the Vaishnava tenets were held by the later Vijayanagar princes of Chandragiri, the chiefs of Venkatagiri, and at the sacred shrine of Tripati. It thus came to be adopted by the European factories, and by the Nawábs of the Carnatic. Conspicuous examples of these are found in the *Star Pagoda* (*vide* pl. xi, 3) of the English East India Company at Madras, and in the *Porto Novo Pagoda* (*vide* pl. xi, 2) believed to have been first coined by the Portuguese at Porto Novo or Feringhipet, and at Arcot under the Nivayat Nawábs of the Carnatic. The huns of Sa'adut Ulla Khán of this type, who succeeded Nawáb Dáwad Khán, and died in 1731, are recognised by the Persian letters (*illah*) on the granulated reverse, which is replaced on those of his relative Safdar 'Ali Khán by the letter (*ain*). On his murder in 1741, the office of Nawáb was conferred by the Nizam on another family, that of Anwar-ud-dín-Khán, but his son Muhammad 'Ali received his investiture direct from Delhi, with the high-sounding title of Walaján Nawáb-ul-hind in 1766. In 1858 I received some information regarding his coinage with extracts of the mint accounts from the Dewán of the late Nawáb. By these it appears Walaján struck coins at other places besides Arcot, viz., Porto Novo, Trichinopoly, and Tiruvamur, and among the coins named are the *Walájahi*, *Kuruki*, *'Umdat-ul-Mulki*, *Star*, and *Feringhipet*.[3] Some of these I have not seen. The *Kuruki* is not uncommon. It has the three standing figures strongly marked, and a plain granulated surface. It and the *Star*, so called from the star impressed on the granulated surface, were probably coined at Tiruvamur, beyond the precints of the English factory, at which place the mint was said to be still standing in 1858. According to the Imperial Gazetteer the Madras mint was built

---

[1] L. c., p. 50.

[2] Numismat. Orient. Coins of Southern India, 1885, pp. 143-4.

[3] The mint records of Hijri 1186 = A.D. 1772 show that the gold coinage was —

Walajáhi	*pagodas*	... ...	$1,870\frac{17}{32}$
Kuruki	„	... ...	$22,654\frac{11}{32}$
'Umdat-ul-Mulki	„	... ...	$995\frac{31}{32}$
Star	„	... ...	$3,81,052\frac{3}{32}$
Feringhipet	„	... ...	$15,098\frac{7}{32}$
		Total ...	$4,21,171\frac{1}{8}$

The silver coinage for the same year was —

Arcot	*rupees*	... ...	7,230	12	9
Tirumavur	„	... ...	2	8	0
Old Pondicherry	„	... ...	0	10	6
		Total ...	7,233	10	15

within the walls of Fort St. George in 1723. But the factory must have exercised the right of coining at a much earlier period, for the Madras Public Records state that consignments of bullion despatched to Fort St. George on the appointment of Sir George Winter as Governor in 1661 were coined into pagodas in the Fort mint, of what denomination, however, is not stated.[1] Also that in 1688 a proclamation was issued forbidding the introduction into the factory of a counterfeit pagoda, fabricated at the Dutch mint of Pulicat [2] "of the same stamp, but not three-quarters the value of ours, which has raised great doubts and scandals upon our coin, to the depreciating it two or three per cent. below Pulicat pagodas, even in our city, by the Merchants and Shroffs to the great prejudice and discredit of our pagodas, and loss of our mint custom: it is therefore agreed and ordered that Proclamation be made in several parts of the town and city, prohibiting all persons whatever from advancing anything upon the Pulicat pagoda by exchange; and whosoever shall offend herein, to pay twenty pagodas for the first fault, and double for the second, and a twelve months' imprisonment for the third. Also that all persons be forbidden to send gold from hence to be coined at Pulicat mint, upon forfeiture thereof upon due proofs; and that the Justices of the Peace do appoint the publishing and affixing these orders in English, Portuguese, and Gentoo at several public places of the city." Still later, during the siege of Fort St. George in 1702, among other conditions of surrender, Nawáb Dáwad Khán demands the surrender of the mint."

In addition to the Three-Swámi and Porto Novo or Scott Pagodas, the old Star pagoda of Madras, or, as it is also called Company varáha or *Puli* varáha, was struck in the early days of the Company, but I am unable to find any reference which indicates its earliest date of circulation. It bears on one side a figure intended apparently for Vishnu with a star above the head, and on the other side a granulated surface with a 5-rayed star (pl. xi, 3). In this coin all public and private accounts were kept, and all dues and salaries paid for a number of years. [3] A brass coin of the same type is contained in the collection of the Madras Museum, to which I can find no reference in the Records, and it is possibly only a fraudulent imitation.

The double and single star pagodas represented on plate xi, figs. 4 & 5 are a more modern development of the old Star Pagoda, and concerning them Dr. Bidie writes: [4] "It is of this

---

[1] Wheeler, *Madras in the Olden Time*, vol. i, p. 32.

[2] As regards Pulicat Pagodas Tavernier says: "Figs. 3 and 4 is the Gold Money which the *Hollanders* coin at *Palicate*, which is a Fort they possess upon the coast of *Coromandel*. Those pieces are also call'd Pagods, and are of the same weight with the others; but for the goodness, I think they are better by two or three in the hundred, than those of the Kings and *Rajas* of the Country, or which the *English* make. I made this observation, being at the Diamond-Mines, and in other parts of the *Indies* where there is any great trade. For the first thing they ask you is, whether you have any Pagods of *Pelicate*; and, if you have, you speed much better in your business." Voyages through Turkey, Persia, and the Indies. London, 1678, pt. ii, p. 6.

[3] See Dr. G. Bidie, *Pagoda or Varáha Coins*. Journ. As. Soc., Beng., vol. 52, 1883, p. 51.

[4] L. c., pp. 51-2.

form that Moor in his 'Hindu Pantheon' says:—"this coin I imagine to be intended for the use of Madras, and cannot but lament that so miserable a specimen of our taste and talents should be suffered to go forth." In designing it the artist seems to have deemed it necessary to give some reason for the name *pagoda*, by putting on the reverse the figure of the gopuram of a Hindu temple, and he then surrounded this with stars to indicate that it was a star pagoda. Again on the obverse, to keep it in harmony with the old forms, he has introduced the figure of a Hindu god, which is apparently intended for Vishnu. There is no date on the coin, but it appears to have been first brought into circulation early in the present century.

Obverse.—The gopuram of a temple surrounded with stars, and the inscription in English "TWO PAGODAS."

Reverse.—Vishnu surrounded with dots, and the inscription "two pagodas" in Tamil and Telugu.

"Counterfeit specimens of this pagoda are very often seen in jewelry, but may usually be easily detected, as in the genuine huns the milling on the edge is oblique like a section of a rope, whereas in the forged ones the milling is like that on modern English coins. The coin as a whole is certainly a hideous production, but curious as perhaps the first departure from a native towards a European type."

There is in the Madras Museum a necklet made up entirely of single pagodas of the last type, but bearing the word DEITY above the gopuram instead of PAGODA, and having a straight milling instead of an oblique milling on the edge. I am unable to find any reference to similar coins, and they must, I think, be regarded as ornamental imitations.

In the year 1642 the first regular despatch was received by 1642.
the Company from Bengal, Mr. Day recommending therein that the Court should establish a station at Ballasore, and declaring that it would be unwise either to neglect or desert the speculation of a trade in Bengal. Four years later the Agent and Council of Fort St. George were raised to the rank of a Presidency.

By the eleventh article of the Treaty of Marriage between 1661.
King Charles II and the Infanta Catherine of Portugal, dated 23rd June 1661, the Crown of Portugal ceded and granted to the Crown of England the Island and Harbour of Bombay, in full sovereignty; and it was understood that this grant would enable the two Crowns to maintain their respective dominions in the East Indies against any future aggressions and encroachments on their subjects and trade by the Dutch Company. On the 27th of March 1668 the King, by Letters Patent, transferred the Island of Bombay from the Crown to the East India Company, granting the Port and Island of Bombay to the London East India Company in perpetuity, "with all the rights, profits and territories thereof, in as full manner as the King himself possessed them, by virtue of the Treaty with the King of Portugal, by which the Island was ceded to his Majesty, to be held by the Company of the King, in free and common soccage, as of the manor of East

Greenwich, on payment of the annual rent of £10 in gold on the 30th September in each year."

As regards the coinage of the Company during the reign of Charles II, Ruding says: [1] "The English merchants trading to the East Indies did in this reign strike silver money in India for the use of their factory at Bombaim, formerly a settlement of the Portuguese, but yielded up to his Majesty upon his marriage with the Infanta of Portugal in 1662. I have not been able to discover the time when the licence to coin this money was granted to the Company, but the earliest of the coins that are known bear date of 1678.

"The earliest coins for the use of the East India Company were either struck by our monarchs, or coined by their authority. Of the former kind were the portcullis pieces of Elizabeth in 1600-1.

"In the reign of Charles II the Company began, by authority from the Crown, to strike silver coins for the use of the factory at Bombay. They were fanams and rupees, all of which bore either the name, or some reference to the sovereign."

Writing further concerning the early coinage of the Company, Ruding says: [2] "Soon after the East India Company obtained territorial possessions in India, it began the exercise of that privilege, which in all countries, and in the East especially, has been considered the right and proof of sovereignty—the coining of money. The circumstances of the Company's coinage were, however, as anomalous as those of the Company itself, which, although to a certain extent possessed of territory, was for a long time obliged to conciliate the native princes, under whom mediately or immediately it held dominion, by professing to acknowledge their supremacy, whilst it still continued necessarily included amongst the subjects of Great Britain. It therefore adopted the policy of seeking the sanction of the Crown to its establishment of local mints; and at the same time it fabricated in these mints coins not in its own name in general, nor with English legends and devices, but in imitation of the established currency of the country, with inscriptions in the Persian or other native language, and in the name of the Emperor of Delhi, or some other Indian prince. The coinage of money on its own account appears to have commenced at Bombay, which island was held in more independence, at first, than any other landed possession. Accordingly in 1671 the Court of Directors gave instructions to their servants at Bombay to establish a mint upon the island, and a few years afterwards the measure was sanctioned by the Crown. A clause in the Charter granted in the 26th year of the reign of Charles II, dated the 5th of October 1677, empowers the East India Company to stamp and coin money at Bombay, to be current wherever the Company's privilege of trade in the East Indies extended, to be called by the name of

---

[1] Op. cit., vol. ii, p. 18, and foot-note, p. 112.
[2] Op. cit., vol. ii, p. 418.

rupees, pices, and budgrooks,[1] and to bear any such seal, impression, and inscription, as the Company should think proper, so that such moneys so stamped and coined should not be called or known by any other name or names of money current in the realm of England or any other part of the British dominions, the East Indies excepted."

Writing during the reign of Charles II concerning the money coined by the English in the Indies, Tavernier says:[2] "Figure 1 and 2 is the money which the *English* coin in their Fort *St. George*, or else at *Madrespatan*, upon the coast of *Coromandel.* They call them Pagods, as those of the Kings and *Rajas* of the country are called. They are of the same weight, the same goodness, and pass for the same value. Formerly the English never coined any silver or copper money; for in some parts that border upon the *Indians*, where they have factories, as at *Surat*, *Maslipatam*, or at *Bantam*, they find it more profitable to carry gold from *England* than silver; gold lying in less room, and not being so troublesome; besides, that by carrying gold they more easily escape the paying those customs which the Kings impose upon gold and silver. But since the present King of *England* (Charles II) married the Princess of Portugal, who had in part of her portion the famous Port of *Bombeye*, where the *English* are very hard at work to build a strong fort, they coin both silver, copper, and tinn. But the money will not go at *Surat*, nor in any part of the Great *Mogul's* Dominions, or in any of the territories of the *Indian* Kings; only it passes among the English in their fort, and some two or three leagues up in the country, and in the villages along the Coast; the country people that bring them their wares being glad to take that money; otherwise they would see but very little stirring, in regard the country is very poor, and the people have nothing to sell but *Aqua vitæ*, made of coco-wine and rice."

With regard to the tin money referred to in the last paragraph, I cannot do better than quote the remarks of Mr. T. G. DaCunha, who says:[3] "Tin coin was current in Portuguese districts round about Bombay, and the English of Bombay issued—it may be for the sake of uniformity—theirs of the same material. The specimens of the latter coinage which have hitherto reached us appear to have been struck between 1708 and 1773, subsequent to the

---

[1] Notes on Budgrook from Yule and Burnell, op. cit.

"Budgrook, s. Port. bazarucco. A coin of low denomination, and of varying value and metal (copper, tin, lead, and tutenague) formerly current at Goa and elsewhere on the Western coast, as well as at some other places on the Indian seas. It was also adopted from the Portuguese in the earliest English coinage at Bombay. In the earliest Goa coinage, that of Albuquerque (1510) the *leal* or *bazarucco* was equal to 2 reis, of which *reis* there went 420 to the gold cruzado."

1638. "They have (at Gombroon) a certain copper coin which they call *Besorg*, whereof 6 make a *Peys*, and 10 *Peys* make a *Chay* (*Shāhī*) which is worth about 5*d*. English."— *V. and Tr. of J. A., Mandelslo into the East Indies*, E.T. 1669, p. 8.

[2] Voyages through Turkey into Persia and the East Indies. Ed., London, 1678, p. 5.

[3] Contributions to the Study of Indo-Portuguese Numismatics. 1880, pp. 24–27.

Mutiny of the Bombay troops under Keigwin, the fusion of the old and new East India Companies into the United East India Company, and the creation of the three Presidencies ruled by Governors in Council, those of Calcutta, Madras and Bombay, each of them absolute within its own limits, until the appointment of a Governor-General for all India in 1773. It is true that, during the time of the Commonwealth, pewter was employed in coining farthings, and some *pattern* farthings of tin were also prepared in the reign of Charles I, and the early part of that of Charles II, which were made current in 1684, and continued to be coined until 1692, when this currency ceased. These dates are, however, too early to account for the existence of the Bombay tin coinage, which appears to be an imitation, from reasons to be mentioned hereafter, of a similar Portuguese mintage . . . . . . It was not only by the adoption of this material for their coinage, but even by the imitation of types and symbols, which were originally Portuguese, that the rising power of the English of Bombay gave a tacit proof of their appreciation of the inventive power of their allies and neighbours, the Portuguese, whose star was now declining, but were still masters of all the districts round about Bombay up to the year 1740. The Portuguese of Chaul had struck a copper *basarucco,* bearing a sheaf of arrows and a bow on the obverse, and the Coat-of-Arms of the Kingdom on the reverse. This coin was issued some time prior to 1577, and must have been current in the environs of Bombay. This device is found engraven on one of the ruined gates of that once famous city. The gate was built in 1577, as testified to by an inscription, a fac-simile of which, with a lithograph representing the gate itself, is inserted in my work on that city.[1] The gate is surmounted by the well-known D. Manuel's terrestrial globe, three arrows in a sheaf, the Coat-of-Arms of the Kingdom of Portugal, and the Cross of the Order of Christ above them all. Here the globe denotes the power, the broad belt which encircles it being intended to represent the conquests and discoveries of the Portuguese throughout the world, and the three arrows tied together peace, which the Portuguese had enjoyed before the building of this part of the fortifications uninterruptedly for thirty long years, which was an unusual occurrence in those troublous times.

Now the three arrows tied together were engraven or represented not only on lithic, but even on numismatic monuments of the Portuguese in India. The English of Bombay copied this emblem on their copper pieces, bearing on one side a crown and on the other three arrows tied together, flanked by the letters *G* and *R* in italic for Georgius and Rex, with the legend *Auspicio Regis et Senatus Anglice* below. To the Portuguese, who appear to have imitated this device from a Spanish coin current in Portugal between 1557 and 1641, called *real de prata*, or 'silver real,' it was an emblem of peace, to the English of Bombay probably a mere ornament, if not a meaningless type."

---

[1] History and Antiquities of Chaul and Bassein. Bombay, 1876, p. 81.

The following types of Anglo-Indian money were issued during the reign of Charles II[1]:—

1. Silver Rupee A.D. 1667.

Obverse.—Within a beaded circle MON. BOMBAY. ANGLIC. REGIMS. A°7°; around A. DEO. PAX. & INCREMENTVM.

Reverse.—A shield with the arms of the Company within a beaded circle; around IND. ORI. HON. SOC. ANG. (pl. xviii, 1).

2. Silver Rupee A.D. 1677.

Obverse.—In centre THE RVPEE. OF BOMBAIM with rosettes; around BY. AVTHORITY. OF CHARLES. THE. SECOND. 1677.

Reverse.—In centre the Royal arms of England in a shield, and a crown above the shield; around KING. OF GREAT. BRITAIN. FRANCE. AND IRELAND.

Coins of the same type were struck, with both plain and milled edge in 1678 (pl. xviii, 2).

3. Silver Rupee. Without date.

Obverse.—A shield of arms between two wreaths.

Reverse.—In centre PAX DEO within a beaded circle; around MONETA BOMBAIENSIS.

(pl. xviii, 5).

4. A half Rupee with device and legends similar to No. 3.

5. A pattern Rupee, in the British Museum, bearing on the obverse a shield of arms similar to No. 3, and on the reverse C.R. 1673.

6. Copper Pice with device and legends similar to No. 1 and, as Atkins suggests, probably from the same die. The character of the letters on the obverse varies somewhat in different coins of this type, the legend being blundered in various ways, and reading, *e.g.*, ONET. ONBAY. NGIƎG. GIM. A coin of the same type is referred to by both Thomas and Atkins, in which the legend reads MOET. BOMBAY. ANGLIC. REG. A°9° (pl. xviii, 3).

7. A copper Cash of the year 1678, bearing on the obverse an orb and cross inscribed 78, and on the reverse some undecipherable native characters, to the interpretation of which I have not been able to find any clue.

8. A Farthing of the year 1674, in the British Museum, bearing on the obverse CAROLVS A CAROLO, and on the reverse REX BRITANNIA, re-struck with the die for the silver rupee No. 2.

9. A lead coin in the British Museum of the year 1678 ?, mentioned by Thomas as having types and legends as in the silver rupees.

10. A pewter (*Zinn*) coin of the year 1675 referred to by Weyl as being of the value of 2 Cash, and having on the observe device and legends similar to the rupee No. 3, and on the reverse 2·75 (pl. xix, 4).

---

[1] *Vide* Weyl, Neumann, Atkins, and an article by Mr. Edward Thomas, F.R.S., in the *Indian Antiquary*, 1882.

11. Silver Coins, bearing on the obverse two C's interlinked, and on the reverse the figure of a deity (Vishnu ?).

Two different sizes of the silver coin of Charles II with the linked C's and figure of a deity, called by Atkins [1] the double and single Fanam, and of the type represented on pl. xi, 11-12, are still met with in the bazaars of Southern India. Of this type coins of three sizes, called respectively the double Fanam, Fanam, and half Fanam, are mentioned by Weyl, who calls the deity on the obverse "der Gott Swami." Another type (pl. xv, 8) of which the Madras Museum possesses specimens, and which I saw for the first time in the British Museum, differing from the preceding in the character of the devices, which are encircled by a ring of dots, was also struck. As regards the source from which the Fanams were issued, they are attributed by Weyl to the Madras Presidency, and Captain Tufnell writes [2] :— "It has usually been attributed to the Bombay Mint, though for the following reasons I am inclined to think it more probable that it is an issue of Madras, coined during Charles' reign. In the first place the *type* of coin connects it with the design imposed by the Vijeyanagar king on the Madras Mint; secondly, it differs entirely from all the known issues struck at the time in Bombay; thirdly, it fits in with the Hindu system of the South; and, lastly, it is occasionally met with in this Presidency, while, from inquiries I have made from collectors in Bombay, I find that it is rarely, if ever, found there."

1686. In consequence of fruitless negotiation for many years to obtain permission from the Native Powers to coin the country money, the Court in 1686 applied to the King for authority to institute a mint for this purpose, and his Majesty (James II) granted a new Charter, dated the 12th April 1686, by which all the former Charters were renewed and confirmed, and power was given the Company to "coin in their forts any species of money usually coined by the Princes of those countries, so that it be made agreeable to the standards of those Princes in weight and fineness, and so that they do not coin any *European* money; and it is declared that all such money so to be coined by them shall be current in any city, town, port, or place, within the limits of the Company's Charters, but not elsewhere." Thus authorised, the Court directed the President and Council of Fort St. George to take particular care that the coins, in stamps, inscriptions, and fineness, should resemble those issued by the Mogul at Rajahmahl, particularly the rupees, it being of inferior moment to offend that sovereign, in this respect, from the war which had been resolved on against his dominions. Application was, at the same time, to be made to the King of Golcondah [3] for

---

[1] Atkins' Coins of British Possessions and Colonies, 1889.

[2] Madras Journal of Literature and Science, 1888, p. 191.

[3] Extracts from a letter from the Company to Fort St. George, dated London, 24th December 1675: "As to the Piscash for the King of Golcondah, if it be not already done, we do hope with it you may obteyn our liberty to coyne silver Rupees and copper Pice at the Fort, which would be a great accommodation in our trade. But in this and all other Piscashes be as sparing as you can."

"Inconvenience having resulted from valuing the Pagoda at 8 shillings and the Rupee at 2s. 6d., order that in future in account the Pagoda be valued at 9 shillings, and the Rupee at 2s. 3d., but the soldiers to receive as many Fanams per Pagoda as of old."

a *Phirmaund*, giving his authority to the Company to coin rupees, and other money in the mint at Madras, and that this money might be current in his dominions; and in all future treaties with the Country Powers, an article was to be introduced, stipulating that the Company's coin should be allowed to be current in their territories. The Presidency of Surat were, further, directed to use such stamps, dies, and tools, as were common in the country, and to issue a coinage, which might facilitate equally the administration of the Company's affairs in Bombay, and their commercial transactions at the ports, where corresponding coins were current. Instructions were also given, relative to the mint at Madras, that this Presidency should make use of the country stamps and dies, under the King's authority, and coin small copper money, proportions of which were to be circulated at Bencoolen.

A silver Rupee of James II was struck in 1687, which bears the following legends and devices :— 1687.

Obverse.—

Centre.— PAX
DEO.

Margin.— BOMBAIENSIS MONETA. 1687.

Reverse.—

*Centre.—*Shield, with the arms of the East India Company (pl. xviii, 4).

During the season 1688-9 the Court received information that 1688-9. a treaty had been made with the Moghul, and that Sir John Child had negotiated a Provisional Convention with Muchtar Khan, the Governor of Surat, by which the Company were allowed to coin money at Surat, in the Moghul's mint-house; but the Court preferred acting on the authority given them by their recent Charter, of having a mint at Bombay, as this would impress the Natives with the importance of the place; and they hoped that, in time, they would be able to supply the Bengal market with rupees coined at Bombay, or, at any rate, exchange their Bombay rupees for those coined at Surat, which would pass current in Bengal, or in any part of the Moghul's dominions. The Court, on this occasion, submitted the question to the consideration of the General, whether the coinage at Bombay ought not to include gold mohurs, as the Company had the Moghul's *Phirmaund*, and the King's Charter, to exercise this branch of delegated sovereignty.

Under the arrangements which were suggested about this time for making Bombay the seat of the Regency, Sir John Child was ordered to be specially attentive to the out-factories on the Malabar coast; the station at Retorah, in the Queen of Attinga's country, was ordered to be fortified, and the factory of Tellicherry strengthened. At the latter place were subsequently minted the silver coins, represented on pl. ii, 1-2 & pl. iii, 2-3, specimens of which in the Madras Museum bear the dates [17] 99 (?) and 1805 respectively. As regards the former of these coins Captain Tufnell says:[1] "I had always looked upon this 99 as being an abbreviated form of the date 1799, but ...... I have seen a small *gold* coin exactly corresponding to the one here described, but with the date 1801 in

---

[1] Madras Journal of Literature and Science, 1888, p. 192.

the exergue, the '99' still appearing at the top." The gold coin of the type here referred to is contained in the collection of the Madras Museum (pl. iii, 4).

1688-9. At this period (1688-9), when the affairs of the Company were generally unsettled, Fort St. George and Madras, which had recently been made a Corporation by Charter, were in a state of tranquillity, the mint was prosperous, and the Company's rupees were in considerable request, though, on account of their intrinsic value, they were melted down by the country people, under the idea of deriving profit from the sale of bullion.

1691. In 1691 the Court ordered the factories at Conimere and Cuddalore to be withdrawn, as a purchase had been made, from the Ram Raja, of a new settlement at Tegnapatam or Fort St. David. The gold coin known as the Porto Novo, Scott, Purunki, &c., pagoda, [pl. xi, 2] appears, says Dr. Bidie,[1] "to have been first struck by the Dutch, and to have had an extensive circulation. Subsequently it was copied by agents of the East India Company, as is evident from the following extract from a letter from the Madras Council to the Deputy Governor of Fort Saint David (near Cuddalore), under date the 21st July 1691.[2] "We doubt the Dutch will make a clamour at your coining their pagodas, and decry them all they can; however, make the experiment, but be sure to equal them in all respects both in fineness and weight and stamp, and we shall give them all the reputation we can here and to the southward, and, could you effect it, currently it would be of great service to the Honourable Company in their trade in those parts, but if you fail you must make another stamp."[3]

1693-5. A copper Cash is referred to by Weyl, and attributed to William and Mary, bearing on the obverse the monogram C.C./E. and on the reverse the date . . 95 (1695 ?); and copper *Faluce* or 20 cash are mentioned by Atkins, bearing on the obverse an orb and cross with the letters C.C./E. within a radiate border, and on the reverse the dates 1693 and 1695, respectively, with a wavy line above and below.

1698. In 1698 the Company acquired a grant from Azim, grandson of Aurungzeeb of Chutanultee Govindpore, and Calcutta,[4] and the fortifications at the latter place were increased, and called Fort William. Four years later the English East India Company and London East India Company, between which there had been great rivalry during the last few years, came to terms under the

---

[1] L. c., p. 51, pl. iii, fig. 21.

[2] *Vide* Garstin's Manual of South Arcot, p. 33.

[3] For further information as to the Porto Novo pagoda, see p. 13.

[4] Notes on Calcutta from Yule and Burnell, op. cit.

1698. "This avaricious disposition the English plied with presents, which in 1698 obtained his permission to purchase from the Zemindar ...... the towns of Sootanutty, Calcutta, and Goomopore, with their districts extending about 3 miles along the eastern bank of the river."—*Orme*, repr. iii, 71.

1702. "The next morning we pass'd by the *English* factory belonging to the old Company, which they call Golgotha, and is a handsome building, to which they were adding Stately Warehouses."—*Voyage to the East Indies by Le Sieur Luillier*, E.T. 1715, p. 259.

1726. "The ships which sail thither (to Hugli) first pass by the English Lodge in Collecatte, 9 miles (Dutch miles) lower down than ours, and after that the French one called *Chandarnagor*." *Valentijn*, v, 162.

title of "The United Company of Merchants of England trading to the East Indies," whose monogram, V.E I.C., is reproduced on many of the copper coins of the last, and early part of the present, century. The London Company agreed to transfer to the English Company, *inter alia*, their rights to all their several forts and factories, within the limits of their Charter, in the East Indies, viz., the factories depending on the Presidency of Bombay; or Surat, Swally, Broach, Ahmedhabad, Agra, and Lucknow; on the Malabar coast, the forts and factories of Carwar, Tellicherry, Anjengo, and Calicut; the factories on the coast of Coromandel, Gingee and Orixa, depending on the Presidency of Fort St. George; on Fort St. George and the City of Madras, Fort St. David, Cuddalore, Porto Novo, Pettipolee, Masulipatam, Madapollam, and Vizagapatam; the factories dependent on the Presidency of Fort William, or Fort William, Ballasore, Chutanultee, Cossimbuzar, Dacca, Hughly, Malda, Rajahmahl, and Patna.

From the Records of the year 1705 it appears that £12,000 in bullion was sent out, to be coined into rupees at Fort St. George, and transmitted to Bengal to clear off all demands, and that President Pitt and his Council were censured for having allowed the demands of certain native merchants to be paid, with interest, without having previously ascertained the frauds, which had been committed by them in making up their accounts, and for having allowed Mr. Tillard to draw on the Court for the amount, at the rate of ten shillings and sixpence, instead of the current rate of nine shillings the pagoda. 1705.

In his Report in 1707 Sir Nicholas Waite, General, Bombay, stated that the Arrack Farms had been placed in the hands of Agents, who were to manage them, because, when put up to sale, no person offered to take them; that the same method had been adopted with the tobacco farms, by which a gain had been made, this season of 22,328 Xeraphins. Concerning this species of money (Xeraphin), which is frequently mentioned in the early transactions of the Company, I cannot do better than quote the following extracts from "Hobson-Jobson":— 1707.

"Xeraphine, Xerafim, &c. The word in this form represents a silver coin, formerly current at Goa and several other Eastern ports, in value somewhat less than 1s. 6d. It varied in Portuguese currency from 300 to 360 *reis*. But in this case as in so many others the term is a corruption applied to a degenerated value. The original is the Arabic *ashrafi*, (or *sharīfi*, 'noble,') which was applied properly to the gold dīnār, but was also in India, and still is occasionally by natives, applied to the gold mohr.

1498. "And (the King of Calicut) said that they should tell the Captain that if he wished to go he must give him 600 Xarifes, and that soon, and that this was the custom of that country, and of those who came thither." *Reteiro de V. da G.*, 79.

1523. "Antonio de Saldanha .... agreed with the said King Turuxa (Turun Sháh) ... that the said King .... should pay to the King our Lord 10,000 Xarafins more yearly .... in all 25,000 Xarafins.

Tombo da India, Subsidios, 79.

1598. "The chief and most common money (at Goa) is called Pardanne Xeraphin. It is of silver, but of small value. They strike it at Goa, and it is marked on one side with the image of St. Sebastian, on the other with 3 or 4 arrows in a sheaf. It is worth 3 testoons or 300 Reys of Portugal, more or less." *Linschoten* (from French ed., 71).

1610. "Imprimis of Seraffins *Ecberi*, which be ten *Rupias* a piece, there are sixtie Leckes." *Hawkins* in *Purchas* i, 217.

c1610. "Les piéces d'or sont cherafins à vingt-cinq sols piece." *Pyrard de Laval* ii, 40.

c1675. "Coins . . . . . of Rajapore. Imaginary coins. The Pagod is 3½ Rupees, 48 Juttals is one Pagod, 10 and ½ Larees is 1 Pagod. Zeraphins 2½, 1 Old Dollar.

"Coins and weights in Goa . . . The *Cruzado* of gold, 12 Zeraphins. The *Zeraphin* 5 Tangoes. The Tango, 5 *Vinteens*. The *Vinteen*, 15 Basrooks, whereof 75 make a *Tango*, and 60 Rees make a *Tango*." *Fryer*, 206.

1727. "Their Soldiers' Pay (at Goa) is very small and ill paid. They have but six Xerapheens per month, and two suits of Calico, stript or chequered, in a year . . . . . and a Xerapheen is worth about sixteen Pence half Peny *Ster*." *A. Ham.* i, 249.

In 1707 the Bengal Council sent to Madras a specimen of the new Emperor, Bahádur Shah's rupee, and desired that all rupees coined at the Fort for Bengal might be made to resemble it, as such coin only would be received or pass in Bengal, whereas at the Fort those rupees could not be circulated for fear, as President Pitt expressed it, of giving offence to Khan Buksh, the apparent King.

During the reign Queen Anne (1702–1714) copper coins were struck, bearing on the obverse the monogram C.C./E. and on the reverse the date. The coins of this type, referred to by Weyl, bear the dates 1702, 1705, and 1709. Copper *Dudu* or *Faluce* (Atkins) were also issued, bearing on the obverse an orb and cross inscribed with the letters C.C./E. within a radiate border, and on the reverse the date, with a wavy line above and below, within a dotted circle. Coins of this type, referred to by Atkins, bear the dates 1702, 1703, 1705, 1706 and 1709. A copper Pice, bearing on the obverse the English crown, and on the reverse the motto [AVSP] I [CIO] REGIS E ASIT AN NGLI, is also attributed by Weyl to the reign of Queen Anne.

1716-17. The Company's presuming to coin money drew down upon them, in the reign of William III. the high displeasure of the reigning Great Moghul, the Emperor Aurungzeeb, whom they had to appease by an explanation. Elphinstone in his "History of India," Vol. II, pp. 555, 556 mentions that A.D. 1693 Khazi Khan was sent to Bombay on this and various alleged delinquencies of the Company, "and that they explained their coining money in their own king's name (which was another complaint against them) by stating that they had to purchase investments at places, where the Moghul's money did not pass."

Marsden in his 2nd Vol. of Numismata Orientalia, p. 663, in his series of the coins of the Moghul Emperors of Hindustan, states:—"It was in this year of Farakhsirs's reign (fifth year, A.D. 1716-17) that the English East India Company obtained from him (through the agency of Mr. John Surman, factor, and Mr. Hamilton, Surgeon, with Khojal Serhad, an Armenian, as linguist) the memorable Firman or Edict exempting them from the payment of customs, authorising them to coin money of the Empire in the Island of Bombay, as had been usual at Chinnapatnam or Madras, and granting them the exercise of many other important privileges." In a note Marsden adds "it is dated the fourth day of the second month (1129), and in the fifth year of the reign (16th January 1716-17)."

A translation of it will be found in Frazer's "History of Nadir Shah," p. 45, and the details of many circumstances respecting it in Scott's "History of Aurangzeeb's successors," p. 139.

Auber in his "Rise and Progress of British Power in India," vol. I. p. 21, gives many particulars of this grant, which, however, Jaffier Khan, the Moghul Governor of India, manifested an indisposition to obey; and, in a despatch from the members of the Embassy, dated Conimbuzar, 15th August 1717, they say "we went ourselves to him, and showed him the Fhermand, and demanded the free use of the mint as before advised." Jaffier put them off, as they say "with a few sweetening words," and by a despatch of the directors, dated 16th February 1721, we find that up to that time the matter still remained as it had been; for then write the directors: "By all this we hope you will lay hold of the present opportunity to get the grants confirmed. First that of the mint." The "present" opportunity was probably the accession of a new emperor (Muhammad Shah), and in 1725 they had obtained the boon; for, in a despatch of the Directors, dated 5th December 1725, they say: "For the reasons by you given we permit you to rebuild your Silver Mint."

In 1717 the Company obtained the island of Diu, 37 townships in Bengal, which gave it the command of the river for 10 mile, S. of Calcutta, and had certain villages restored to it near Madras, which had formerly been given by the Arcot ruler, and resumed. The earliest coins of the Company in the Madras Museum which bear a date are a thick copper coin bearing on one side the monogram of the Company, and on the other the date 1722, and a smaller thin coin likewise bearing the monogram, and the date 1733. Coins of the latter type were also issued by the Dutch East India Company, bearing their monogram, V.O.C. (*Vereinigte Ostindische Compagnie*), to which a letter was frequently added, representing the initial letter of the mint town, e.g., P (Pulicat) and N (Negapatam).

The following copper or lead (*Zinn*) coins are attributed to the reign of George I (1714–1727):—

1. Lead. Double and single Pice—

Obverse.—The English Crown with G.R. above, and BOMB below.

Reverse.—The motto AVSPICIO REGIS ET SENATVS ANGLIÆ.

[pl. xvi, 8].

As regards lead coins of this type (of which the later issues bear the dates) struck during the reigns of the Georges, the writer of an article in the Numismatic Chronicle remarks [1]: "Ruding . . . gives engravings of a large lead piece from Bombay, which has no date, but, from the letters G.R. on it, he assigns it with probability to George I. I have a similar coin with the date 1741, weight

[1] Vol. xviii, p. 76.

1 oz. 6 grs., and another with date 1771, weight 15 dwts. 15 grs, and I have seen two pieces of similar type and metal half their size. The coins of 1741 came to me from Dublin: that of 1771 was found a few years since at Kinsali in repairing a house. These three specimens in lead, being of the reigns of George I, II, and III, from their succession, would seem to indicate some established and continuous purpose. It is unlikely that anything honorary would be struck in so worthless and easily injured metal as lead; yet, as they all bear the authoritative inscription "Auspicio Regis et Senatus Angliæ," we may presume, in the absence of any information, that they were current coin."

2. Copper Pice. Without date—
Obverse.—The English Crown with G.R. above, and BOMB below.
Reverse.—The motto AVSPICIO REGIS ET SENATVS ANGLIÆ.

3. Copper Pice. 1714—
Obverse.—The Company's bale mark, and date 1714.
Reverse.—A lion right, within a dotted circle.
Coins of this type, of three sizes, are contained in the collection of the British Museum (pl. xix, 5, 6, 7).

4. Silver three, double, and single Fanams, presumably struck for the Madras territories:—
Obverse.—Orb and cross inscribed, with the letters C.C. E. within a dotted circle.
Reverse.—An undecipherable Indian inscription within a dotted circle.

[pl. xix, 1, 2].

5. Copper coins with device and legends similar to No. 4.

[pl. xix, 3].

"In 1725," says Sir Walter Elliot,[1] "the attention of the factory was attracted to the coinage of the rupee. It appears that the profits gained at the Madras mint on the coinage of silver had encouraged the issue at the native mints at Arcot, St. Thomé, and Covelong, of rupees inferior in standard, but of the same nominal value, so as to divert the flow of bullion from the Company's mint to their own. This led to stringent regulations prohibiting the export of bullion from the Factory, and to a reduction of the mint charges." On this subject Mr. Wheeler says[2]: "The first important matter which received the attention of Governor Macrae was that of the coinage of rupees at the Madras mint. It seems that the Native chiefs had awakened to the profit derived by the Madras Government from the coinage of rupees; and accordingly they had not only set up mints of their own, but, about this time, they contrived to make more rupees out of the same quantity of silver, than were made by the Company. For instance out of every hundred ounces of silver, the mints at St. Thomé and Arcot turned out to the merchant Rupees 266, annas 14; whilst the mint in Fort St. George only turned out Rupees 257, annas 7. Thus the merchant obtained nine rupees seven annas more for his hundred ounces of silver at St. Thomé and Arcot than he could

---

[1] Op. cit., p. 145.
[2] Op. cit., vol. ii., pp. 387—92.

obtain at Fort St. George. In other words the Madras rupee was 2 per cent. dearer than the rupee of Arcot or of St. Thomé. The consequence was that the merchants preferred coining their silver at the latter mints; and the Company found its custom decreasing. Accordingly Governor Macrae directed Messrs. Pitt, Benyon and Emmerson to enquire into the whole matter ...... It will be seen by the following resolution that Governor Macrae endeavoured to put matters to rights; 1st—by prohibiting the export of silver from the Company's bounds, and thus compelling the merchants to coin their silver at Fort St. George; 2nd—by lowering the Company's custom ½ per cent. and the mint charges ½ per cent., or altogether 10 rupees per thousand. Henceforth then the custom and charges at Madras would be 30 rupees per thousand; whilst the custom and charges at St. Thomé, Arcot, and Covelong would be nominally 21 rupees per thousand, but actually 31 rupees 11 annas per thousand. The original entry will serve to render the subject more intelligible.

"Monday, 8th March 1725. Messrs. Pitt, Benyon and Emmerson deliver in a report of the coinage, together with an account of the charges and customs collected at our mint, and those in the country; as likewise an account of the produce of a hundred ounces of silver of the fineness of the rupee in our and St. Thomé mints.

"This matter being fully debated, it was upon the whole agreed that no silver except rupees shall be permitted to be exported to any part of the coast of Coromandel under penalty of confiscation, half to the informer and half to the Company; and the Secretary do give notice hereof at all the public places in the town.

"As by the calculates and reports abovementioned, it appears that our rupee is two per cent. dearer to the merchants than the St. Thomé and Arcot rupee, it was further argued that we ought to find out some method to lessen the charge of coinage, that so we may bring it nearer to a par with the country coin; and it appearing that the Brahmins actually indisburse 11¼ rupees per thousand, and that they must have something besides for their trouble, it was plain their custom could not be reduced above a ½ per cent., which not being sufficient, it was agreed to strike off a half per cent. likewise from the custom paid the Company; which it is hoped will be approved by the Honorable Court of Directors for the following reasons:—

"First, that the present charge of coinage being 4 per cent. in our mint, and but 21 per thousand in the St. Thomé mint, nobody will bring any silver to us, but on the contrary carry it away thither; but that when our custom is reduced to three per cent., the difference will be so much less that probably we may have the greatest part of the coinage return to us, especially since our rupee is in greater esteem in the country than theirs.

"Secondly, that we shall receive orders from Europe in two years; and if our Honorable Masters shall disapprove hereof, which we cannot believe they will, it may be laid on again.

"Thirdly, that at present the revenue is sunk to almost nothing, so that should no more silver be coined here than has been for sometime past, the difference will be very inconsiderable; whereas should we hereby regain the coinage it will be very apparently advantageous to the Company.

"Lastly, that the Company will save ½ per cent. in the coinage of their own silver; which, as we coin one-third generally of what goes down to the Bay, will very near if not over compensate for the reduction of the custom on other silver.

These being the causes why it is thought necessary to lessen the charge of the coinage, it was recommended to the President to talk with the mint Brahmins, and bring them to an agreement for lowering the charge agreeable to the above resolve, which he accordingly promised."

To the time of George II, who reigned from 1727 to 1760, the following copper and lead coins must be referred:—

1. Copper double Pice.
Obverse.—The English crown, with G.R. above, and BOMB below.
Reverse.—The motto AVSPICIO REGIS ET SENATVS ANGLIÆ and the date (pl. xix, 8.)

2. Copper Pice—
Obverse.—The English Crown, with G.R. above, and BOMB and the date below.
Reverse.—The Bale mark of the Company.

3. Copper half Pice with device and legends similar to No. 2.

4. Copper quarter Pice of a similar type, but without the date, are referred to by Atkins.

5. Copper Pice (*Weyl*)—
Obverse.—The Company's shield.
Reverse.—The date 1742 (pl. xx, 1, 2.)

6. Copper Pice. (*Weyl*)—
Obverse.—The Company's shield.
Reverse.—MON. BOMB 1745 (?).

7. Copper Pice, bearing the Company's shield on both obverse and reverse.

8. Copper Cash.
Obverse.—The Bale mark of the Company.
Reverse.—The date (pl. i, 2, 4.)
The earliest date on coins of this type in the Madras Museum is 1733.

9. Copper *Dudu* or *Faluce* (Atkins)—
Obverse.—Orb and cross inscribed with the letters C.C. E. within a radiate border.
Reverse.—The date, with a wavy line above and below, within a beaded circle. [pl. i, 6, 7, 8].

10. Copper half Faluce of the same type as No. 9.

11. Lead double Pice.

Obverse.—The English crown, with G.R. above, and BOMB below.

Reverse.—The motto AVSPICIO REGIS ET SENATVS ANGLIÆ, and the date. [pl. xvi, 8.]

12. Lead Pice of the same type as No. 11.

The following extract from the notice of a Meeting held on Saturday, 5th September 1730, throws light on the origin of the "M. Pagoda." "At that Meeting the President observing to the Board what is recommended in the last general letter concerning the badness of pagodas, desires this affair may now be taken into consideration, and that the Assay Master may be sent for to assist with his advice. Mr. Weston was accordingly called in, and acquaints us that the pagodas grow daily worse; and that some he tried in May last were no better than eighty-three and a half touch; whereas they ought to be of the value of the Negapatam pagodas, which is eighty-five and three-quarters. The Board taking into consideration the danger the Company's estate is in, and that commerce must inevitably suffer if this uncertain money circulates longer unsuspected; and that, though we defer taking proper measures to prevent this abuse at present, at last there will be an absolute necessity to do it (may be, when it will give a much greater shock to trade); and likewise no time can be so proper as when the Company's cash is so low as now by the large draught sent to the Bay by the "Cadogan." We therefore come to the following resolution, in order to secure the Company's estate, which we hope will be sufficient to open the eyes of everybody else, who must otherwise be undone by their credulity. 1730.

"That a new pagoda be coined of equal weight and fineness with the Negapatam pagoda, and with the same stamp, only distinguished with the letter M on each side the image; which shall be current in all branches of the Company's business, and that no other sort shall be paid or received, except in the Northern investments, where the old Madras pagoda is only current. But as this resolution cannot be put in practice till we have a supply of gold from China and elsewhere to make a circulation, we declare that this order of the Board shall not be in full force till the First of May ensuing; when we are in hopes the Eastern ships will be returned, and the merchants have sufficient time to coin the gold they purchase into the abovesaid specie; which were we to insist upon before a supply arrives, they must be obliged to melt down the present coins, and be considerable losers in giving it a new stamp."

"From these extracts," says Sir Walter Elliot,[1] "compared, with the information of the Dewán, it appears that these Vaishnava *húns* were struck at the same time by the English, the Portuguese, and perhaps the Dutch, as well as by the Nawábs of Arcot, and though bearing the same name, were not confined to the same mints. Thus the *Star*, *Kuruki* and *Porto Novo* were struck equally at the factory and the Nawáb's mints, the latter being

---

[1] Op. cit., p. 145.

situate, according to the Factory records, at Arcot, St. Thomé and Covelong, but according to the Dewán at Arcot, Tiruvamur, and Porto Novo. By St. Thomé and Covelong are probably meant the obscure village of Tiruvamur. The *Porto Novo hûns* I apprehend to have been first produced by the Europeans at that place, whence it came to be also designated as Feringhipet. When the influence of the Portuguese on the Coromandel coast was circumscribed by the Dutch and the Muhammadans, the mint appears to have passed into the hands of the Nawáb, who continued to issue *hûns* under the name of *Porto Novo, Feringhipet, Negapatam* (where had also been a Portuguese Factory), and afterwards of *Scot pagodas*. Buchanan found in 1800 that at Pálghát "the accounts were kept in *Feringy* or *Porto Novo pagodas* or varahuns; *pudamoni*[1] commonly called vir ráya fanams, and *cash*," and that there was a profit in bringing *Porto Novo pagodas* from Dhárapuram in Coimbatore to Pálghát, and carrying back *vir ráya* fanams."

1742. The following letter from Mr. Sidney Foxall, dated Fort St. George, 16th August 1742, furnishes us with a description of the process employed in the coinage of money in the Madras Mint at that time:—

"Honorable Sir and Sirs,

"It is a great concern to me to observe by an extract of the General Letter from England, that the Honorable Company should have the least shadow of reason to suspect that I have been any way negligent in my duty towards them; for I do assure your Honors, that I have at all times used my utmost care and diligence, as much as in me lay, to keep the minters to their weight and standard in all the moneys that have been coined since my time; and that I never discovered any attempt to adulterate the coin, but in the affair of Rangum with which I took care to acquaint this Honorable Board.

"The methods of coinage in the Tower of London differ much from what is used here; it being impossible to adulterate the gold and silver there after the Assay Master has tried them, being cast into bars, before the assays are taken. Those bars afterwards run through flatting mills, the money cut out with an engine, milled and stamped, but no more melted. The constant method here has been, first to melt the gold or silver, and break it into small grains or powder; the muster is taken by the Assay Master; after which (if of the proper standard), the grains or powder is distributed among a great number of coolies in several work-houses or godowns: who weigh every rupee and pagoda separate, and afterwards deliver them to other coolies to melt. Different persons receive them to flat, and others to stamp. By which method of working, your Honors must be very sensible, that, if it was not for some confidence which must be put in the undertakers, and the fear of punishment in such as should be detected, my utmost care and vigilance could not prevent from adulterations. The only check upon them, and what I frequently

[1] *Pudamoni*, signifying new coinage, so called in contra-distinction to the *palaya mani* or ancient coinage.

make use of after the first trial, is to take muster of their moneys in their presence, to assay after it is finished, to let them see I have a watchful eye over them.

"What I have already said, with the present flourishing state of the mint, will I humbly hope induce my Honorable Masters to believe that I have not been any way negligent in my duty hitherto, and shall take my utmost care that they have no cause of complaint in future.

"I am,

"Honorable Sir and Sirs,

"Your most obedient and humble Servant,

"SIDNEY FOXALL."

Writing in 1794 concerning the method employed in coining money at the Bombay Mint at that time Lieutenant Moor says:[1] "Tippoo, from his coins being regularly stricken and milled, must have a regular die, which is an apparatus unknown in other parts of India. In Bombay there is no mechanical process either for ascertaining the value of the piece, or of giving it the impression. The manner is as follows: the metal is brought to the mint in bars the size of the little finger, where a number of persons seated on the ground provided with scales and weights, a hammer, and an instrument between a chissel and a punch: before each man's birth is fixed a stone by way of anvil. The bars are cut into pieces, by guess, and if, on weighing, any deficiency is found, a little particle is punched into the intended rupee; if too heavy, a piece is cut off, and so until the exact quantity remains. These pieces are then taken to a second person, whose whole apparatus consists of a hammer and a stone anvil, and he batters them into something of a round shape, about seven-eighths of an inch diameter, and one-eighth thick; when they are ready for the impression. The die is composed of two pieces, one inserted firmly into the ground, the other, about eight inches long, is held in the right hand of the operator, who squatting on his heels (the posture in which all mechanics and artists work; the posture, indeed, in which every thing is done in India, for if a man has a dram given him, he finds it convenient to squat upon his heels to drink it), fills his left hand with the intended coins, which he with inconceivable quickness slips upon the fixed die with his thumb and middle finger, with his forefinger as dexterously removing them when his assistant, a second man with a mall, has given it the impression, which he does as rapidly as he can raise, and strike with the mall on the die held in the right hand of the coiner. The diameter of the die is about an inch and a half, inscribed with the Great Moghul's names, titles, date of the Hejra, his reign, &c., but as the coins are not so large, they do not, consequently, receive all, nor the same impression. The rupee is then sent to the treasury, ready for currency, as no milling, or any farther process is thought necessary."

In 1742 a grant of liberty to coin Arcot rupees was given to the Company, and the following is a translation of a Sunnud under

[1] Narrative of Little's Detachment, App. note ii, pp. 499, 500.

the seal of Nabob Sadutalla Khan Bahadur, Subah of Arcot, dated the 4th November 1742 :—

"To the Mutasadar of the country of Chennapatnam and Sircar of Trippasoor, belonging to the Carnatic of Golcondah and to their successors.

"Be it known unto all men that from the beginning of the year Fusly 1152, I have ordered a mint to be erected to coin pagodas and rupees in Chindadrepettah, belonging to Chinnapatnam; and the same to be under the power of Mr. Benyon, Governor of Chennapatnam, for the Company. Wherefore do you let the said Governor have and enjoy for the Company all the customs that may arise in the said mint. Observe this as a strict taukeed and perform it accordingly. Dated Ramazan 17th in the 25th year of the reign of the Great Mogul Mahomed Shah."

Translation of the contents written on the back of the foregoing Sunnud.—"Ordered that a mint may be erected in Chindadreepettah belonging to Chinnapatnam for coining pagodas and rupees, and it may be commenced from the beginning of the year Fusly 1152, and to be under the power of Mr. Benyon, Governor of Chennapatnam, for the Company.

"His Excellency's order by his handwriting is to draw a Sunnud to the following purpose:

"'That Andiappah Naick, Dubash of the Governor of Chennapatnam, represented that the Governor desires liberty to erect a mint in Chindadreepettah belonging to Chennapatnam for coining pagodas, rupees, &c., and that we should free them from paying us the customs arising thereby, and let the same be applied to the said Governor for the Company; a sunnud is granted for that purpose."

Entered in the Book 19th Moon Ramazan, in the 25th year of the reign of the Great Mogul Mahomed Shah, which is the 4th November 1742.

1746. In 1746 a French fleet, commanded by La Bourdonnais arrived off Madras, which surrendered, but was restored to the English by the treaty of Aix-la-Chapelle two years later.

1756. In 1756 Siráj-ad-daula (Surajah Dowlah), then a youth of only eighteen years, marched upon and took Calcutta with a large army, but the city was retaken by Clive and Watson at the beginning of the following year. "The establishment of an independent coinage in Bengal," says Ruding,[1] "was of later date than at the other presidencies. For some time subsequently to their purchase of the zemindary of Calcutta, the only indulgence granted to the Company was the privilege of having their bullion coined at the mints of the Nawab of Bengal, which were at Patna, Dacca, and Murshedabad. After the capture of Calcutta a right to establish a mint of their own was one of the stipulations in the treaty with Suraj-ad-Doula, dated 7th February 1757."

1758. In 1758 Clive was appointed by the Court of Directors the first Governor of all the Company's settlements in Bengal. After a war, which continued fitfully for many years, Colonel (afterwards Sir Eyre) Coote won the decisive victory of Wandewash over the

---

[1] Op. cit., vol. ii., p. 418.

French General Lally and invested Pondicherry, which capitulated in 1761.[1]

In the year 1760 George III came to the throne. Many of the coins struck during his long reign (1760-1820) are still met with in large numbers in the bazaars, but the following copper and lead coins are worthy of special reference on account of their scarceness:— 1760.

1. Copper Double and Single Pice.
   Obverse:—The English crown, with G.R. above, and BOMB and the date below.
   Reverse:—The Bale Mark of the Company. (pl. xv, 1).

2. Copper half Pice. Of the same type as No. 1.

3. Bombay Pice.
   Obverse:—The Bale Mark of the Company.
   Reverse:—1 PICE BOMBAY, and the date (1773 and 1777). (pl. xv, 3).

4. Copper half Pice.
   Obverse:—The Bale Mark of the Company.
   Reverse:—½ (pl. xix, 9).

5. Lead double Pice.
   Obverse:—The English crown, with G.R. above, and BOMB below.
   Reverse:—The motto AVSPICIO REGIS ET SENATVS ANGLIÆ, and the date.

6. Lead Pice. Of the same type as No. 5.

7. Lead half Pice.
   Obverse:—The Bale Mark of the Company.
   Reverse:—½ PICE. (pl. xix, 10).

8. Lead quarter Pice. Of the same type as No. 7, but with the value ¼.

9. Copper quarter Pice.
   Obverse:—C.G. 1813.
   Reverse:—PI ¼ CE.
   (pl. xx, 3).

10. Copper. Two Annas.
   Obverse:—PATNA POST TWO ANNAS and the date.
   Reverse:—Value of the coin in Persian.

11. Copper. One Anna.
   Same as No. 10, except the value ONE ANNA.
   (pl. xx, 8).

---

[1] Notes on Pondicherry from Yule and Burnell, op. cit.

"Pondicherry. This name of what is now the chief French settlement in India, is *Pudu-ch'chēri*, 'New Town,' more correctly *Pudu-vai*, C.P.

Brown however says it is *Pudi-cherū*, 'New Tank.' The natives sometimes write it Phulcheri."

1780. "An English officer of rank, General Coote, who was unequalled among his compeers in ability and experience in war, and who had frequently fought with the French of Phoolcheri in the Karnatik, and had as often gained the victory over them......" *H. ob. Hyder Naik*, 418.

1763. On the 15th of January 1763 Major Carnac, who commanded the English forces, marched against the prince, Sháh Álum, and attacked and beat him. "He pursued the prince very closely for some days, till the latter found himself so straightened, that he offered to throw himself upon the protection of the English, which was accepted, and on the 8th of February he joined the English camp, and proceeded with them to Patna. The province of Allahabad, including the district of Corah, estimated at the yearly revenue of twenty-two lacks of rupees, was assigned to him in guarantee by the Company; and, in addition, to render his establishment splendid, the British Governor, in behalf of the Company, agreed to pay into his Majesty's treasury the annual sum of twenty-six lacks of rupees from the revenues of Bengal." [1]

Describing a rupee of Sháh Álum struck in 1176 (A.D 1762-3), and bearing on one side the inscription

ضرب کلکته سنه جلوس ... ۴

"struck at Calcutta in the 4th year of the auspicious reign," Marsden says: [2] "This rupih was evidently struck at the period when Sháh Alum, after the defeat of his army, consented to place himself under the protection of the English Government, and to receive an assignment of certain revenues for his support. It is perhaps the earliest that expresses the name of Calcutta, and its weight accords with the regulated standard. The work is creditable to the new mint."

1765. In 1765 it was agreed by the articles of a Treaty and Agreement concluded between the Governor and Council of Fort St. William on the part of the English East India Company and the Nabob Nudjum ul Dowla "that the books of the Circar shall always be kept, and the business conducted at Moorshedabad, and that shall as heretofore be the seat of my government, and wherever I (Nabob Nudjum ul Dowla) am, I consent that an English gentleman shall reside with me to transact all affairs between me and the Company, and that a person of high rank shall also reside on my part at Calcutta to negotiate with the Governor and Council.

"I will cause the rupees, coined in Calcutta, to pass in every respect equal to the Siccas [3] of Moorshedabad, without any deduction of Batta; and whosoever shall demand Batta shall be punished. The annual loss on coinage, by the fall of Batta, on the issuing of the new Siccas, is a very heavy grievance to the country; and after mature consideration, I will, in concert with the Governor and Council, pursue whatever may appear the best method for remedying it."

---

[1] Francklin's History of the Reign of Sháh Álum, p. 25.

[2] Numismat. Orient., 1825, pt. ii, p. 677.

[3] Note on the word Sicca from Yule and Burnell, op. cit.

"The term *Sicca* (sikkha, from Arab. *sikka*, 'a coining die,'—and 'coined money,'—whence P. *sikka sadan* to coin) . . . ."

1683. "Having received 25,000 rupees Siccas for Rajamaul."—*Hedges*, MS., April 4.

1705. "Les roupies Sicca valent à Bengale 39 sols."—*Luillier*. 255.

1779. "In the 2nd Term, 1779, on Saturday, March 6th, 'Judgment was pronounced for the plaintiff. Damages fifty thousand Sicca rupees."

On the 12th of August 1765, the Emperor Sháh Álum granted to the Company "the Dewanee of the provinces of Bengal, Behar and Orissa as a free gift and Ultumgau, without the association of any other person, and with an exemption from the payment of the customs of the Dewanee, which used to be paid by the Court . . . ."

In 1765 pattern gold mohurs, half, and quarter mohurs, were struck, bearing on the obverse a shield and the inscription ENGLISH EAST INDIA COMPANY, and on the reverse the inscription BOMBAY 1765. These pattern pieces (pl. xx, 4) I have seen in the collections of the British Museum and Mr. H. Montagu. In 1770 a pattern gold mohur was struck, bearing on the obverse the inscription BOMBAY 1770 15 RUPS, and on the reverse a Persian inscription. (pl. xx, 5.)

In 1767 commenced the first of the Mysore wars, of which the 1767.
last terminated with the capture of Seringapatam and death of Tippoo Sultán in 1799. The interesting fact is mentioned by Lieutenant Moor[1] with reference to a Bombay half pice coined in England for the use of the island, on which is the Honorable Company's mark, that "this mark is put upon everything that the Company send to India, and Tippoo, seeing it on their musquets, has imitated it on his; and on the butt, lock, barrel, and bayonet, is the mark, in which, instead of V.E.I.C., *United East India Company*, we see *Hydr*, Tippoo's father's name, in Persian. He put it also upon his cannon."

In his work "The principles of money applied to the present state of the coin of Bengal," Sir James Steuart says: "It has been observed that this coin, called gold mohurs, had been formerly coined at Delhi, of the same weight and fineness with the Sicca rupee of Bengal and other countries of Hindustan; but that they passed conventionally, having no legal *denomination*. In 1766 . . . . . it was proposed as an expedient for augmenting the currency of specie to make a coinage of gold . . . . . . , and the directors of this operation, pitching upon fifteen Arcot rupees as the value of one gold mohur, instead of estimating the value of these fifteen Arcot rupees by the fine metal contained in them, estimated them by their current value, which was above the proportion of their intrinsic worth. Not satisfied with this first deviation from principles, they added to the mohur (already over-rated in its proportion to the fifteen silver Arcot rupees) no less than 8 per cent. extra denomination, entirely arbitrary. So when this gold currency came abroad, it proved to be no less than 17½ per cent. worse in payments than silver rupees of Bengal, Madras, Bombay, and Surat.

"The people of that country (Bengal) had been so long accustomed to silver coin, that they never would, except when forced to it, receive the mohurs in payment. So the Company was obliged to make a new regulation in 1769, little better than the former. At last the gold currency fell altogether to many per cent. below its intrinsic value."

---

[1] Narrative of Little's Detachment, App. p. 478, pl. ii, 14, 15.

In his 'Voyages to the East Indies' I. Splinter Stavorninus, Rear Admiral in the service of the States General, says [1] of the coinage of Bengal, which presidency he visited between the years 1768 and 1771: "The only current coins in *Bengal*, and the whole extent of *Indostan*, are gold and silver rupees. All foreign gold and silver, whether coined or in bullion, is carried to the mint, and transformed into rupees, which are stamped with Persian letters instead of any portrait or arms. They decrease every year in value, and at the end of nine years the *sicca* rupees are taken at the same rate as *Arcot* rupees. When the rupees first come from the mint, they are called *sicca* rupees of the first year. Those which are coined at *Moorshedabad* are the current coin in which the trade of the Company is carried on, and by which all the other rupees in circulation here are reduced. It is divided into sixteen *annas*; its intrinsic value in Dutch money is one gilder, four stivers and a half, and it is taken in the Company's books at twenty-five stivers; but in Indian currency at thirty-one stivers and a half, for which it is current at *Hougly*. It is the money of account, according to which the value of the other rupees is calculated at a discount or agio, which is called *batta*, of from six to twelve per cent., which undergoes continual fluctuations, by the management of the money-changers. The *Arcot* rupees, which are coined by the English at *Arcot*, and by the French at *Pondicherry*, go for thirty stivers, yet the last are reckoned from one to three per cent. better than the former.

"The gold rupee, which is called *mohur*, is worth fifteen silver *sicca* rupees.

"Halves, fourths, eighths, and sixteenths of rupees are likewise coined; the last, as above said, are called *annas*.

"Copper coin is not seen in *Bengal*. For change they make use of the small sea-shells called cowries,[2] eighty of which make a *poni*, and sixty or sixty-five *ponis*, according as there are few or many cowries in the country, make a rupee. They come from the *Maldive* Islands. The money-changers sit upon all the *bazars* with quantities of them to furnish the lower orders with change for the purchase of necessaries. One hundred thousand rupees make what is called a *lack*, and one hundred lacks or ten millions of rupees a *crore*."

As regards the coinage current at Surat Stavorninus says: [3] "The coins that are current here are of gold, silver, and copper.

---

[1] Ed. London, 1798, vol. i, p. 460.

[2] Note on cowries from Yule and Burnell, op. cit.

1753. "Our Honorable Masters having expressly directed ten tons of cowries to be laden in each of their ships homeward bound, we ordered the Secretary to prepare a protest against Captain Cooke for refusing to take any on board the Admiral Vernon." M. *Long*. 41.

1780. "We are informed that a copper coinage is now on the carpet...... it will be of the greatest use to the public, and will totally abolish the trade of cowries, which for a long time has formed so extensive a field for deception and fraud." Hicky's *Bengal Gazette*.

1803. "I will continue to pay without demur, to the said Government, as my annual peskush or tribute 12,000 *kahuns* of cowries in three instalments as specified herein below." *Treaty Engagement* by the Rajah of Kitta Keonghur, a tributary subordinate to Cuttack, 16th December 1803.

[3] Op cit., vol. iii, p. 8.

The coin of gold of the country is the *mohur*, which is gold of twenty-three carat; it goes here for fifteen silver rupees, though its value is not constantly the same, but is settled according as gold is at a high or at a low price. All foreign gold coins are only taken according to their weight and intrinsic value.

"Ducats are likewise met with here, but no one is obliged to receive them in payment contrary to his inclination; they are distinguished into three sorts: the Venetian ducats, which are worth from $4\frac{1}{4}$ to $4\frac{5}{16}$ rupees, or f. 6-7 to 8 stivers; all other European ducats, to which they give the appellation of *images*, and which are current at from $4\frac{1}{8}$ to $4\frac{3}{16}$ rupees, or f. 6-3 to 5 stivers; and the third or last sort, those of *Constantinople* or *Stambouli*, among which are comprehended all other Turkish, Arabian, and Persian ducats, and which go at from $3\frac{7}{8}$ to $3\frac{15}{16}$ rupees, or f. 5-16 to 18 stivers. The value of these coins is lowered or enhanced in proportion as more or less gold is imported.

"The silver rupee is the standard coin of the country, the only one which is struck in the empire of Hindostan, and is current all over it; its real value in Dutch money is scarcely four and twenty stivers, but here, among the Europeans, it is calculated at thirty stivers; every rupee contains sixteen *annas*, but the calculation by *annas* is not so common here as in *Bengal*; the fractions of rupees are generally settled by *pice*, which is the only copper coin here, and of which more or less go to a rupee in proportion as copper is at a low or at a high price; when I was at Surat, sixty-four *pice* were given for a rupee; it is said that there are also leaden *pice*, but I saw none of them.

"In the same way as cowries are made use of in *Bengal*, as the lowest medium of exchange, almonds, which are called *badams*, are employed for that purpose here; the comparative value whereof is, as may easily be conceived, more liable to variation than any other representative medium.

"No other money is current here, and all foreign coins are taken according to their weight and assay; but the Mexican dollars, or pieces of eight, known among the natives by the appellation of *raal lakria*, must, if weight, contain seventy-three *waals*: their value is uncertain, running from f. 318 to f. 324 per hundred, and some times, but seldom, a little higher."

A double rupee, bearing the date ۱۱۹۳ (A.D. 1780), is described by Marsden[1] bearing on the obverse the inscription

سکه مبارک عالم گیر بادشاه غازی

and on the reverse the inscription

ضرب مچهلی پٹن سنه جلوس ۲۱

"Struck at *Mechli-pattan* (Masulipatam) in the 21st year of the auspicious reign," concerning which he says: "This extraordinary coin presents a still more unaccountable anomaly than any that has yet been noticed in the produce of the Anglo-Indian Mint. The numeral characters for the year 1194 are distinct, and, with due regard to consistency, it is of the 21st year of the reign, which can be no other than that of *Shâh Alum*. But it bears the

[1] Numismat. Orient., 1825, part ii, p. 685.

name (and his only) of *Alum-gīr* ; being either that of his father, who reigned not quite six years, and was put to death in 1173, or of the great *Aureng-zéb*, who died in 1118. Whether this discreditable anachronism proceeded from inattention or design, it would now be difficult to ascertain. The piece is a well executed double rupih, coined at a city within the English jurisdic-
1792-4. tion on the Coast of Coromandel, usually named Masulipatam."

In the years 1792—4 the following proof copper coins, which never came into circulation, were struck :—

1 and 2. Pice and Half Pice.

Obverse :—The Bale mark of the Company with the date 1792 below.

Reverse :—A balance with the word عدل between the scales.

These coins are hexagonal in shape.

3. *Obverse* and *Reverse* :—The Persian legend سکہ کونپنی ۱۷۹۳ عیسوی in the centre within a thick rim incused ENGLISH EAST INDIA COMPANY.

The edge is inscribed with the legend ENGLISH UNITED EAST INDIA COMPANY. (pl. xx, 6).

4. *Obverse* :—The crest of the Company with the value 48 TO ONE RUPEE and the motto AUSPICIO REGIS ET SENATVS ANGLIÆ incused upon a thick rim.

Reverse :—Similar to No. 3.

No. 5. *Obverse* :—The Bale mark of the Company with the date 1794 below.

Reverse :—سکہ کونپنی ۱۷۹۳ عیسوی without a thick rim, or English legend.

1793. In 1793 a regulation was passed, by which the gold and silver coin in Bengal, Behar, and Orissa was reformed, and the currency of any gold or silver coin in those provinces, but the nineteenth sun gold mohur, and their respective division into halves and quarters was prohibited.

In this regulation it is stated that "upon the mints at Patna, Dacca, and Moorshedabad being withdrawn soon after the commencement of the Company's administration, the proprietors and farmers of land in the interior parts of the country, who were bound by their engagements to pay the public revenue in sicca rupees, experienced considerable difficulty in obtaining those rupees from the coinage of them being confined to Calcutta, at which place the only mint that remained in the provinces was established ; they were, in consequence, compelled to collect the rents from the ryots in the species of sonaut, or other old rupees, of which there happened to be the greatest number in their respective districts, and which they were permitted to pay into the public treasuries at a fixed exchange. In consequence of the ryots being required to pay their rent in a particular sort of rupee, they of course demanded it from the manufacturers in payment for their grain or raw materials; whilst the manufacturers, actuated by similar principles with the ryots, required the same species of rupee from the traders who came to purchase their cloth or other commodities. The various sorts of old rupees, accordingly, soon became the established currency of particular districts ; and, as a necessary consequence, the value of each rupee was enhanced in the district in which it was current, from being in demand for all transactions. As a further consequence, every other sort of rupees brought into the district was rejected, from being a different measure of value from that by which the inhabitants had become accustomed to estimate their property ; or, if it was received, a discount was exacted upon it, equal to what the receiver would have been obliged to pay upon exchanging it at the house of a shroff for the rupee current in the district, or to allow upon passing it in payment to any other individual. Thus if a sicca rupee of the nineteenth sun, which is intrinsically worth about seven per cent. more than an Arcot, was offered in payment in the Dacca Province, it was either refused, or received nearly at the same value as an Arcot; whilst the holders of Arcots, or other sorts of rupees, who carried them into districts in which they were not current were subject to similar loss ...... The money-changers are the only description of people who derive any benefit from this disordered state of the coin. The loss falls upon Government and the public at large, and must be perpetual, unless the various old and counterfeit rupees now current in the different parts of the country can be thrown out of circulation, and one species of rupee made the general standard measure of value in all transactions between individuals and between Government and its subjects. The sicca rupee of the nineteenth sun is the established coin of the country, and the rupee in which the public revenues are payable. It was with a view to render it the general measure of value, that Government determined, in the year 1773, that all rupees coined in future should bear the impression of the nineteenth sun or year of reign of the Sháh Alum, and no other species of rupee (with the exception of some Arcots) has since been coined in the Calcutta Mint. The rupees of the eleventh, twelfth, and fifteenth sun were indeed directed to be considered current equally with the nineteenth sun sicca rupee ; but this was a temporary measure, intended to be continued in force only until there should be a sufficiency of the nineteenth sun sicca rupee introduced into circulation ....The preceding remarks evince, that it is in the interest of individuals of every description, except the money-changers, to co-operate with the Government to render the nineteenth sun sicca rupee generally current, and the standard of value throughout the country. Among the measures considered necessary to effect this important object, the following were the principal : First, to direct the officers employed in the provision of the investment, and manufacture of salt, and all commercial transactions of the Company, to make their agreements with individuals for sicca rupees of the nineteenth sun.........Secondly, to oblige individuals to estimate their property by the nineteenth sun sicca rupee.........Thirdly, to prohibit the receipt of any rupees, excepting siccas of the nineteenth sun, at the public treasuries after the date above alluded to........Fourthly, to establish mints at the cities of Patna, Dacca, and Moorshedabad, to coin precisely the same rupee as that struck at Calcutta........ By the operation of these rules the various sorts of old and light rupees must, in course of time, fall to their intrinsic worth compared with the sicca of the nineteenth sun, as they will produce no more in the mint, and to which they will necessarily be brought to be converted into siccas, as they will be nowhere passable or in demand as coin, from being nowhere a measure of value. The rules by which the gold coin has been regulated have been productive of evils, similar to those which have prevailed with regard to the silver coin. Under the native administration, and until the year 1766 the gold mohur was not considered as a legal tender of payment in any public or private transaction, nor was the number of rupees for which it was to pass current ever fixed by the Government. It was struck for the convenience of individuals, and the value of it in the markets fluctuated like other commodities, silver being the metal which was the general measure of value throughout the country. In the year 1766, the value of the gold coin with respect to the silver was first fixed, and the former coin declared a legal tender of payment. A gold mohur was struck and ordered to pass for fourteen sicca rupees. But as this coin (calculating according to the relative value of the two metals) was much below the worth of the silver in the number of rupees for which it was ordered to pass, it was found impossible to render it current, and it was accordingly called in, and a new gold mohur, being that now current, was issued in 1769, which was directed to pass as a legal tender of payment for sixteen sicca rupees. The intrinsic worth of this coin was estimated to be equal to the nominal value of it, or as nearly so as was deemed necessary to render it current at the prescribed rate. But whether owing to the effect of the orders for the introduction of the over-rated gold coin of 1766, the considerable value of the new gold mohur, and the want of divisions of it, so as to render the coin calculated for the dealings of the lower orders of the people in the interior part of the country, or other causes, the currency of it has been almost entirely confined to Calcutta, where it has been received and paid in all public and private payments at the fixed value of sixteen sicca rupees. But this partial currency of the gold coin has enabled the money-changers to practice an abuse upon the public and individuals of a nature similar to that which has prevailed regarding the silver ....The means which appear best calculated to render the gold mohur generally current are to declare it receivable at all the public treasuries and in all public payments throughout the provinces, at the rate of sixteen sicca rupees; to make it a legal tender of payment in private transactions; to coin a great proportion of halves and quarters; and lastly, to impose a duty upon all gold bullion sent to the mint to be coined so as to prevent too large a proportion of gold being introduced into circulation, by diminishing, in some degree, the advantage at present derived from the importation of it in preference to silver."

To guard, as far as possible, against the counterfeiting, clipping, drilling, filing, defacing, or debasing the coin, it was enacted by Section VII of Regulation XXXV that "the edges of both the gold and silver coin are to be milled, and the dies are to be made of the same size as the coin, so that the whole of the impression may appear upon the surface of it."

As regards the coins of the nineteenth sun, which are repeatedly referred to in the above Regulation, Marsden says[1] in the course of his observations on a gold mohur, bearing on the obverse the date 1197 (A.D. 1781-2), and on the reverse the inscription

ضرب مورشداباد سنه جلوس ... ١٩

"struck at Moorshidábád in the 19th year of the auspicious reign."

"The legend adopted by Sháh Alum at his succession is continued on this *muhr* and the subsequent coinage in gold and silver, professing to be from the mint of Murshidábád, the modern capital of the province of Bengal, but which, in fact, were executed at Calcutta, under the immediate authority of the East India Company's Government. So early, indeed, as the year 1757, we find a treaty with the Nabob *Serajáh ed-daulah*, in which it is stipulated that sikkas (rupihs) may be coined at Allenagore (*Allah-nagar?*) or Calcutta, in the same manner as at Murshidábád. A similar article appears in a treaty with Jafir Ali Khán in 1763, and with Najim ed-daulah in 1764; but all these were superseded by the treaty of 1765, negociated by Lord Clive, then Governor of Bengal, in which a grant is made to the Company by Sháh Alum, of the Déwáni or plenary collection and administration of the revenues of that province. This *muhr* of 1196, as well as the nearly similar pieces of 1197, 1198, and 1201 are, in point of workmanship, respectable coins, and exceed in weight, by about 20 grains, the ancient gold of the empire; but present a fresh instance of that total disregard of the consistency and fidelity of dates, which has been already noticed as marking the money struck under European control; for although actually the coinage of the twenty-third, twenty-fourth, and twenty-eighth years of the monarch's reign, as indicated by the corresponding years of the *hejrah*, they all express uniformly the *nineteenth* year. This anachronism, repeated through every successive coinage of the same mint, has confounded the investigations of writers on Indian numismatics, and cannot be too strongly reprobated." This "anachronism," or "glaring absurdity," as it is also called by Marsden, is referred to by T. C. Tyschen[2] in the following words:—

"Mira est in his numis annorum imperii cum annis Hegiræ discordia: etenim cum Schah Alem regnum inierit a 1175, annus ejus 19 erat Heg 1193. Contra annus Heg 1202 esset imperii 28 a 1203, imp. 29 . . . . Videntur Angli typis veteribus aversæ partis aliquando uti, de annis miseri imperatoris rectè numerandis parùm curiosi. Further Mr. Stanley Lane-Poole says in the Introduction to the Coins of the Sultáns of Dehlí in the British Museum[3]: "Daulat Khan Lódí and Khizr Khán, in the general confusion which accompanied the invasion of India by Timúr, preferred rather to trade upon the traditional credit of their predecessors than to make any demands upon the people's trust in their personal solvency, and thus issued their coins in the name of Fíróz III or Muhammad III, the mints of which issues cannot be held to offer a very trustworthy evidence of the extent of their striker's dominion, which, however, we know from other sources

[1] Numismat. Orient., 1825, part ii, p. 688.
[2] De Numis Indicis Comment, p. 192.
[3] 1884, p. xvii.

to have been limited to a small district immediately surrounding Dehlí. Neither of these two puppets was a king in any real sense, and to such it mattered little whose superscription was placed on the public money,—his duty was confined to authorising the legality of the new issues by so much of his attestation as was implied in the annual date recorded on the reverse . . . . . a system, indeed, which the East India Company, of their own free will, imitated with much credit and simplicity by striking their rupees in the name of Sháh 'Álum and other defunct monarchs of Dehlí whose money had of old obtained good repute in the local bázárs. But as the progressive annual dates, which were needed to test the good faith of Oriental princes, came in process of time to be a source of confusion and an opportunity for money-changers, the Government adopted the expedient of selecting the best current coin of the day and based their standard upon its intrinsic value; and so the immutable date of the XIX *san* (year) of Sháh 'Álum came to figure upon our much prized 'Sicca Rupees.'[1]"

A rupee is described by Marsden,[2] bearing on the obverse the inscription

سکه زد بر هفت کشور سایه فضل اله
حامی دین محمد شاه عالم پادشاه ۱۱۹۹

and on the reverse the inscription

ضرب کلکته سنه جلوس ... ۲۳

concerning which he says: "It seems extraordinary that at the period when a handsome, well-executed coinage of gold and silver was issuing from the Mint of Calcutta (though nominally from that of Murshid-âbâd), a rupih so rude as this should make its appearance in the same capital . . . . . Another specimen of the same coinage, on which the year of the era is obliterated, has the twenty-fifth year of the reign; as has the half rupih of the same class, weighing 3 dw. 17½ grains." Concerning a gold mohur struck in the name of Sháh Alum in 1202 (A.D. 1787-88) he says[3]: "In the workmanship of this coin we observe the first instance of milling on the edges in the European manner. There is a difference also in the style of engraving the characters, which have here a flat surface."

As regards the several varieties of coin produced by modifications of weight, standard, or die, from time to time in the Calcutta and subordinate mints of the Bengal Presidency, which bear the same legend and date, the following mode of discriminating them is pointed out by Prinsep[4]:—

"(1) The old standard sikká rupee of 1793—1818 has an oblique milling.

"(2) The new standard sikká rupee of 1818—1832 has a straight milling.

---

[1] E. Thomas: *Chronicles*, pp. 329, 330; *International Numismata Orientalia*, vol. i, part 1; *Ancient Indian Weights*, p. 53 f.

[2] L. c., p. 689.

[3] L. c., p. 690.

[4] *Useful Tables*. Ed. by Edward Thomas, 1858, pp. 2, 3.

"(3) The new sikká rupee, struck under the present regulation, has a plain edge without milling, and a dotted rim on the face.

The distinctions of the oblique and straight milling apply also to the old and new gold mohur.

Of the up-country or Farrukhábád coins—

"(4) The old standard Farrukhábád rupee (or '45th Sun Lucknow rupee' of Regulation XLV, 1803) has an oblique milling.

"(5) The Benares rupee, coined 1806—1819, has also an oblique milling.

"(6) The new standard Farrukhábád rupee, coined at the Farrukhábád Mint, 1819—24, and at the Benares Mint, 1819—30, and now at the Ságar Mint, has an upright milling.

"(7) The Farrukhábád rupee, coined under the new regulation at the Calcutta Mint, has a plain edge, and a plain rim on the face.

"The coins struck before 1793 at the old mints of Patna, Murshidábád, and Dacca, the Benares rupee anterior to 1806, and the coins of all the native independent states, are known by their having no milling. The Company's coin up the country is thus generally called *kaldár*, 'milled or made by machinery,' in contradistinction to the unmilled or native coins, which are fashioned and stamped with the hammer and anvil."

About the same time as the passing of Reg. XXXV, 1793, the Surat rupee of the Moghul Emperor was adopted as the currency of the Bombay Presidency. By an agreement with the Nawáb of Surat the rupees coined by both were to circulate at par, and they were mutually pledged to preserve its standard. The Nawáb's rupees, however, were soon found to contain 10, 12, and even 15 per cent. of alloy; in consequence of which the Bombay rupees were melted down, and recoined at Surat; the coinage of silver in the Bombay Mint was suspended for twenty years, and the Súrátis alone were seen in circulation. At length in 1800 the Company ordered the then Surat rupee to be struck at Bombay, and thenceforth it became fixed at 179 grains' weight, 164·74 pure. The mohur was also equalised in weight thereto.

By Regulation XLV of 1803 it was enacted that— 1803.

(Section II). A silver coin, to be denominated the Lucknow sicca rupee of the forty-fifth sun (pl. vii-1), struck in the mint of Furruckhabad, corresponding in weight and standard with the sicca rupee at present struck at Lucknow, in the dominions of the Nawáb Vizier, and thence denominated the Lucknow rupee, is hereby declared to be the established and legal silver coin in the provinces ceded by the Nawáb Vizier to the English East India Company.

(Section IV). A mint shall be established at, or in the immediate vicinity of the town of Furruckhabad, in which Lucknow sicca rupees of the forty-fifth sun, and of the prescribed weight and standard, and half and quarter rupees of the same standard and proportionate weight, will be coined.

(Section V). The Lucknow forty-fifth sun sicca rupee, as established by this regulation, shall be of the same size and form as the nineteenth sun sicca rupee, struck in the mint at Calcutta, and shall bear the following impression :—

Obverse

الہ حامی دین محمد سایہ فضل شاہ عالم بادشاہ سکہ زد بر ہفت کشور

Reverse

میمنت مانوس سنہ ۲۵ جلوس ضرب فرخ آباد

(Section VI). The half and quarter rupee shall be proportionately less in size than the rupee according to their respective value, and shall bear the same impression as the rupee.

(Section XII). The Mint Master at Calcutta shall cause a private mark to be put on all dies, which may be prepared for the mint at Furruckhabad, but in such a manner as not to be distinguishable by the naked eye, or by persons unacquainted with it. These marks shall be varied as often as the Mint Master at Calcutta shall judge proper upon new dies being made.

1811. In 1811 a coinage from Spanish dollars took place at the Madras Mint, consisting of double rupees, single rupees, halves and quarters, and one, two, three, and five fanam pieces. A silver coinage of half and quarter pagodas of dollar silver fineness also took place then. The silver half pagoda weighed 326·73 grs. troy, and was equal to 1¾ Arcot rupee.

1812. The following statement, dated Fort St. George, 24th April 1812, shows the denomination of gold and silver coins manufactured in the Madras Mint from April 1807 to December 1811 :—

Gold.

Double Pagodas.
Single ,,

Silver.

Half Pagodas.
Quarter ,,
Five Fanams.
Double ,,
Single Fanams.
Double Rupees.
Single ,,
Half ,,
Quarter ,,
One-eighth ,,
Four annas.
Two ,,

The five, double, and single fanam pieces, are thin coins, but there is in the Madras Museum collection a thick five fanam piece (pl. XVI, 9) with oblique milling, and a thick double fanam is mentioned by Atkins. These coins are very scarce, and are either, as has been suggested, of older date than the others, or were struck as patterns.

The English inscription on the coins is sometimes blundered, reading, *e.g.*, DOUBLE FANVM OF EANAM.

The silver four-anna and two-anna pieces are now exceedingly scarce, and a two-anna piece is referred to by Atkins as having been probably fabricated about the same time, in which the English inscription is in script character.

In a proclamation, dated Fort St. George, 19th June 1812, it is stated that "the coinage of double rupees, half and quarter pagodas has ceased, but these coins shall still continue to pass in circulation, and be issued and received at all the public treasuries at the same rate and value as heretofore.

"The coinage of rupees, half rupees, and quarter rupees of English standard fineness shall be commenced at the mint of this presidency forthwith, and shall severally weigh as follows, and contain the following proportions of pure silver and of alloy. The rupee shall weigh 180 grains English troy weight, and shall contain $166\frac{1}{2}$ grains of pure silver, and $13\frac{1}{2}$ grains of alloy. The half rupee shall weigh 90 grains English troy weight, and shall contain $83\frac{1}{4}$ grains of pure silver, and $6\frac{3}{4}$ grains of alloy. The quarter rupee shall weigh 45 grains English troy weight, and shall contain $41\frac{5}{8}$ grains of pure silver, and $3\frac{3}{8}$ grains of alloy.

"The above rupees, containing each $\frac{8}{400}$ of a grain more of pure silver than the Arcot rupees which have been issued from the Madras Mint under the proclamation of the 15th of July 1807, half rupees and quarter rupees shall pass in general circulation, and shall be received and issued at all the public treasuries under this presidency at the same rate with the Arcot and Company's rupees now in circulation, that is, at 350 rupees to 100 star pagodas."

A letter to the Chief Secretary to Government, dated Fort St. George, 7th January 1813, states that "considerable quantities of the new rupees, halves, and quarters, having now been coined, the issue of two-anna pieces from the mint will shortly commence ..... We are of opinion that the two-anna pieces, though hitherto unknown in the circulation of this presidency, will readily incorporate with the existing currency; integral numbers of these coins measuring with the pagoda, half pagoda and quarter pagoda, as well as with the rupees and its sub-divisions of halves and quarters. Thus twenty-eight two-anna pieces are equivalent to one pagoda, fourteen to the half, and seven to the quarter pagoda." 1813.

The term *Soolakie* or *Soolackie* as applied to coins is explained by a letter to the Chief Secretary to Government, Fort St. George, dated 18th January 1813, wherein it is stated that "there are two modes of rendering coins Soolakie ..... The one is adopted for the most part by the petty village surrafs in those territories (the Nizam's) who, being in general very inexpert in ascertaining the fineness of the metal, invariably punch a hole in the rupee to convince themselves that it is good silver; but as this expedient is not sufficient to guard against the frauds of coiners, who frequently counterfeit rupees of copper covered with a coat of silver, with one or two such holes in them, it is usual for the surrafs, when they have the slightest suspicion that the metal is base, to punch a fresh hole in it. In consequence, it is by no means uncommon to see rupees with eight or ten such marks indented upon them. The other kind of Soolakie coins are made so by the surrafs of large towns who undertake to *shroff* the money belonging to individuals for a certain percentage, under an agreement to make good any coins that may afterwards turn out to be counterfeit. In order that the coins that have undergone such examination may be recognised, each principal suraff has a private stamp or mark of his own, which he affixes to the edge or some other part of the coin. The existence of one or more such marks gives a sort of sanction to the currency, as the credit of those who have put their stamp to it is a pledge for its goodness. Hence many rupees have forty or fifty such impressions, and at last become completely defaced. Neither of these modes of making the rupee Soolakie diminishes at all the weight of it, but, according to long custom, its value in exchange becomes greatly reduced when it is imported into the Company's territories."

It appears from a letter addressed to the Board of Revenue by the Collector of Tinnevelly that by an old order of Government it was provided that all payments made to the troops in that province should be solely in *Cully* fanams (which are stated to have been coined originally by the Hindu Government in that province) at the fixed exchange of sixteen and a half per star pagoda. This order was rescinded in the course of the year 1812.

The following list is of interest as showing the various kinds of gold and silver coins which were melted and recoined at the Madras Mint in the years 1807 to 1813[1]:—

Timmanaidoo	Pagodas.
Sultawny	,,
Vencataputty	,,
Doorgee	,,
Jemsherry	,,
Feroke	,,
Ahamuddy	,,
Aununtaroy	,,
Madras	,,
Sunnakurk or Madras	Pagodas.
Mittee or ,,	
Porto Novo	Pagodas.
Bahadari	,,
Pulliput	,,
Siddeke	,,
Timmanaidoo Half	Pagodas.
Sharkany	,,
Gajaputty	,,
Darvady	,,
Naidoo Pertaup	,,
Subderally	,,
New Subderally	,,
Commengy	,,
St. Thomé	Pagodas.
Kurky	,,
Atchootaroy	,,
Elephant	,,
Ekary	,,
Old Ekary	,,
Old Mahomed Shaye	,,
New ,, ,,	,,
,, Hurpanully	,,
Old ,,	,,
,, Sravanore	,,
New ,,	,,
Old Arnee	,,
Vandavash	,,
Pulicat	,,
Vencataputty	,,
Bombay	,,

Bunder	Pagodas.
Cacanadie	,,
Rassee Rapadum	,,
Poondanull and Longvet	,,
Pulk Bunder Kurky	,,
Peddatala Bengalore	,,
Star Pagodas soldered with rings.	
Sataury or Sravanaroy Pagodas.	
Tanjore	Fanams.
Rauket or Aparunjee	,,
Rassee	,,
Timmanaidoo	,,
Canteroy	,,
New Veroy	,,
Old ,,	,,
Aununtaroy, Double	,,
,, Single	,,
Gopally	,,
New Gopally	,,
Old ,,	,,
Travancottah Cully	,,
Arealore	,,
Woodiary	,,
Cully	,,
Chuckree	,,
Calicut	,,
Tinnavelly	,,
New Gold Mohur.	
Old ,,	
One-third Old Gold Mohur.	
,, New Gold Mohur.	
Sunnamola	Mohur.
Bombay	,,
Akburry	,,
Dilhe	,,
Rassee	,,
Soorat Jayanagur	,,
Sultauny	,,
Wallace	,,
Poonah	,,

[1] The spelling is retained as it occurs in the Mint Records.

Venetions or Shanar Cash.	Chellavany Rupees.
Alkoss Cash.	Narrain Pettah ,,
Guinea Cass.	Company's Soolaky ,,
Mydores.	Cunnanore ,,
St. Thomé Cash.	Gurnamully ,,
Gold Rupees.	Sultauny ,,
Spanish Dollars.	Emaumy ,,
Cut ,,	Chandoly ,,
German Crowns.	Masulipatam ,,
American Dollars.	Bombay ,,
Duccatoons.	Elephant ,,
Pondicherry Rupees.	Half Pagodas.
,, ,, 2nd sort.	Quarter ,,
Soolaky ,,	Sravanore Rupees.
Arcot ,,	Sicca ,,
Nabob Arcot ,,	Arcot ,,
Arcot Soolaky ,,	Bunder ,,
Nokurrah ,,	Kaukenadoo ,,
Mysore ,,	Pulicat ,,
Mallarthaye ,,	Four Annas.
Sunnamola ,,	Bungapully Rupees.
Soorat ,,	Chuckrums.
Rassee ,,	Tellicherry Fanams.
Adony ,,	Various other ,,
Kurnal ,,	

Under the heading July 21, 1813, Ruding says[1]: "The coins which usually circulated in the East Indies had not, as it appears, received any sanction from Government, until an Act which was passed at this time declared it to be expedient for the protection of property and trade in the East Indies, that, etc., etc.; and also that further provisions should be made for the punishment of the crimes of, etc., etc., and of counterfeiting the current coin, and uttering such counterfeit coin in the East Indies; it therefore enacted that if any person within the local limits of the criminal jurisdiction of any of His Majesty's Courts at Fort William, Fort St. George, Bombay, or Prince of Wales' Island, or if any person, personally subject to the jurisdiction of the said courts, at any place in the East Indies, or any place between the Cape of Good Hope and the Straits of Magellan, where the United Company of Merchants of England trading to the East Indies should have a settlement, factory, or other establishment, should counterfeit, or procure to be counterfeited, or willingly act or assist in counterfeiting any of the gold or silver coins of any of the British Governments in India, or any gold or silver coin usually current and received as money in payments in any part of the British possessions in the East Indies, it should and might be lawful for the court, before which any such person should be convicted of any such offence by due course of law, to order and adjudge that such person should be transported to such place beyond the seas, and for such term of years as the said court should direct. The punishment for uttering such counterfeit coin, knowing it to be such, to be upon conviction, for the first offence six months' imprisonment with hard labour during that time at the discretion 1813.

1. Op. cit., vol. ii, p. 111.

of the court, and surety to be given for good behaviour for six months more, to be computed from the end of the first six. For the second offence two years' imprisonment with hard labour as before, and surety to be given for two years after the expiration of the term of imprisonment. For the third offence transportation for life. A certificate, under the hand of the proper officer of the court, to be a sufficient proof of the former conviction.

"On conviction (upon the oath of one or more credible witness or witnesses, before one of His Majesty's justices of the peace, or if there should be no justice of the peace duly qualified to act in the place where such offence should be committed, before one of his majesty's court there) of having in possession more than five pieces of such counterfeit coin, without lawful excuse, the proof of which to lie upon the party accused, the whole of such counterfeit pieces to be forfeited, and to be cut to pieces and destroyed, and the offender to pay for every such piece not more than forty, nor less than twenty sicca rupees, in the currency of the place where such offence should be committed; one moiety of which to go to the informer or informers, and the other moiety to the poor of the presidency, settlement, or place where such offence should be committed, and in case the penalty should not be forthwith paid, the offender to be committed to the common gaol or house of correction, there to be kept to hard labour for the space of three calendar months, or until such penalty should be paid."

1815. In the 17th clause of a Regulation enacted 31st March 1815 for establishing certain rules for the business of the Madras Mint, it is stated that: "The coins now fabricated in the Madras Mint are of the following denominations: of gold *double pagodas*, each weighing three pennyweights, nineteen grains, and seven-eleventh parts of a grain, troy, of English standard, and of the value of two pagodas; *single pagodas*, each weighing one pennyweight, twenty-one grains, and nine-eleventh parts of a grain, troy, of English standard, and of the value of one pagoda: of silver *single rupees*, each weighing seven pennyweights and twelve grains, troy, of English standard, and of the value of twelve fanams sixty-eight cash, and four-seventh parts of a cash; *half rupees*, each weighing three pennyweights and eighteen grains, troy, of English standard, and of the value of six fanams, thirty-four cash, two-seventh parts of a cash; *quarter rupees*, each weighing one pennyweight and twenty-one grains, troy, of English standard, and of the value of three *Fanams*, seventeen cash, and one-seventh part of a cash; and *two-anna* pieces, each weighing twenty-two and a half grains, troy, of English standard, and of the value of one fanam, forty-eight cash, and four-seventh parts of a cash.

The inscriptions on the single and half rupee were—

Obverse

۱۱۷۲ سکه مبارک بادشاه غازی عزیزالدین محمد عالم گیر

Reverse

ضرب ارکاٹ سنه ٦ جلوس میمنت مانوس

The inscriptions on the quarter rupee and two-anna piece were—

Obverse

۱۱۷۲ سکہ عالم گیر بادشاہ

Reverse

سنہ ٦ ضرب ارکاٹ

In a letter from the British Resident at Bangalore, dated 13th September 1816, concerning the Surat Rupees in circulation in the Province of Mysore it is stated that: "The Surat Rupee was originally imported into the Mysore country by the troops of Hyder Ali Khan, and by the soucars who returned from Malabar with his army after the capture of Calicut in or about the year 1766, but the currency was very limited until the conquest of Seringapatam, when that coin became somewhat more common in these provinces. As there was not any considerable commercial intercourse between Malabar and Canara and Mysore for several years after the fall of Seringapatam, the amount of the circulation in Soorat Rupees was never extensive until 1808." 1816.

In 1817 considerable correspondence took place as to the establishment of a mint by the French Company at Pondicherry. It was proposed that, with a view to simplifying accounts and removing any inconvenience which might arise from the establishment of the French Mint, the rupees to be coined at Pondicherry should be of precisely the same weight and value as those struck at Madras and at that time current in the territories of the Honorable Company. But to this proposition the Madras Government replied to the effect that it seemed scarcely necessary to express the expectation of the Governor-General in Council that the impression on the French coin should be such as to render it easily distinguishable from the coinage of the British Government, and that, were the mintage at Pondicherry to be after the pattern of the coins struck by the British Government, as there seemed grounds for imagining might have been in contemplation, the British Government would in effect be made to answer for the intrinsic work of a currency, which it would have no means of regulating. In conformity with the instruction of the British Government, the following specimens of the coins struck at Pondicherry were forwarded by the British Consul on June 12th, 1817:— 1817.

One Rupee.
Half ,,
Double Fanam.
Single ,, of which
eight were equivalent to a Rupee.
Half Fanam.
One Doodee.
Half ,,
One Cash, of which
sixty-four were equivalent to a Fanam.

A letter from the Director of the Pondicherry Mint, bearing the same date, states that "I have the honor to send you eight specimens of the species (of coins) we have coined since the restoration of the place of Pondicherry to the French Government, viz.:—

"One Rupee. A small crescent has (ever) been added to the stamp as a mark of its being a French Rupee.

One Half Rupee.
One Double Pondy Fanam.
One Single " "
of which eight make a Rupee.

One Half Pondy Fanam.
One Doodoo or Quadruple Cash.
One Half Doodoo or Double Cash.
One Single Cash, 64 of which make a Fanam.

"We have not yet coined any gold species. The French old pagoda or crescent pagoda has the same weight and the same degree of fineness as the Star Pagoda. Many years before the Revolution the Mint of Pondicherry had ceased coining crescent pagodas. It had confined itself to coining 'three Sawmy'[1] Pagodas, otherwise improperly called Madras Pagodas.

"They were designed for the trade of Punjum cloths at our factory of Yanan. This last kind of species we will probably coin in a short time."

With respect to the crescent, which is mentioned in the above letter as being marked on the Pondicherry rupee, the British Commissioner remarks in a letter, dated 7th May 1817: "Adverting to a former letter respecting the French coinage, wherein I stated that the legend on it would be entirely different from that on ours, I beg to observe that the information I then conveyed to you was obtained in conversation with Count Du Puy and M. Dayot. The French coinage being now current in Pondicherry, I perceive that the legend is the same, or nearly so, as that of the Company's rupees, and that the principal mark of distinction is a small crescent on one of the sides. The intrinsic value of the coin I understand to be somewhat greater than that of ours."

By Regulation XXV of 1817 "for fixing the weight of the pice struck at the Calcutta mint, and for giving general circulation to pice struck at any of the mints subordinate to this presidency," the copper paisá struck at the Benares mint, weighing 98½ grains, which were intended at first for circulation in the province of Benares only, and were distinguished with a trident or trisúla, were made current throughout the Bengal provinces at par with the Farrukhábád paisá.[2]

The following extracts from the Minutes of Consultation, dated 16th September 1817, bear upon the proposed new gold and silver coinage: "In considering this important subject," it is stated,

---

[1] Pagode a trois figures.

[2] Notes on *pice* or *paisá*. From Yule and Burnell, op. cit.

C. 1590. "The dám...... is the fortieth part of the rupee. At first this coin was called *paisah*."—*Ain.*, 31.

1615. "Pice, which is a copper coyne; twelve drammes make one pice. The English shilling, if weight, will yeeld thirtie-three *pice* and a halfe." *W. Peyton* in *Purchas*, 1, 530.

1673. "*Pice*, a sort of copper money current among the poorer sort of people...... the Company's accounts are kept in book-rate *pice*, viz., 32 to the mam. [*i.e.*, mamoodie] and 80 pice to the rupee." *Fryer*, 205.

1689. "Lower than these (pice) bitter almonds here (Surat) pass for money, about sixty of which make a *pice*." *Ovington*, 219.

1726. "1 *ana* makes 1¼ stuyvers or 2 *peys*." *Valentijn*, v. 179.

"the Board have referred particularly to the letter from the Honorable Court, dated the 25th of April 1806, which contains the ground-work of all their subsequent orders concerning it. In that letter the Honorable Court explained their object to be to establish a general currency for the whole of India. They stated that the standard currency forming the money of account ought to be of one of the precious metals only, but not to the exclusion of the other; that the metal ought to be silver; and that no ratio ought to be fixed between the standard silver coin and the gold coin, but that gold should be left to find its own value. The Court further desired that the gold coin should be denominated a gold rupee,[1] and that the gold and silver rupees should be the same in weight, fineness, form and inscription. They also desired that half and quarter gold and silver rupees, and annahs should be coined, and stated that a copper coinage of six-pice, three-pice, and one-pice pieces would be sent from England.

"The Mint Committee report that they are aware of no objection to the immediate execution of the arrangements proposed by the Honorable Court, and they accordingly recommend that, with the exception of single annahs, the gold and silver coinage should forthwith commence in pursuance of the Honorable Court's orders. They propose also that the rupee should become the money of account, and that the accounts of Government should be converted from gold into silver at the present ratio of 1 to 13·875, or one pagoda for three rupees and a half. The money of account at Madras has heretofore been the gold pagoda, which used also to form the actual currency. When the silver rupee was introduced into the currency, it was settled that three rupees and a half should represent one pagoda. In consequence of the pagoda being undervalued at that rate, it has gradually disappeared from circulation, and the rupee now forms the actual currency, and, though not the money of account, has become the standard of value.

"With respect to the form and impression of the new gold and silver coins, these will finally be settled either in Bengal or in England. As the currency is intended for general use throughout India, it will be deserving of consideration whether the impression ought not to be in English, and whether the form ought not to resemble that of English rather than of Indian coins."

A proclamation, dated Fort St. George, 9th December 1817, states that "The Right Honorable the Governor in Council, in furtherance of the orders of the Honorable the Court of Directors, is pleased to publish for general information, that hereafter the standard circulating medium is to be the Madras silver rupee, in which all issues of pay and allowances, civil and military, and all public contracts are to be reckoned, made, and executed, and that the coinage of star pagodas will hereafter be discontinued.

---

[1] There is in the Madras Museum a single specimen of the little coin (pl. xi-10), which is commonly called the Bombay gold rupee, concerning which Marsden says (Num. Or., 1825, pt. ii., p. 696): "Of the same year of the reign (of Sháh Álum, 1218 or 1219), and evidently from the same mint, are some very small gold coins, weighing each about 12 grs., and which must be considered as gold *ánás* or sixteenth parts of a *muhr*. In appearance they resemble rather the gold fanams of the Karnatik, than fractional denominations of Hindustani coins."

"The Right Honorable the Governor in Council is also pleased to declare that all pay and allowances, both civil and military, having been heretofore rated in pagodas and converted into Arcot rupees at 350 per 100 star pagodas shall continue to be the same, and that all payments made from the public treasuries, and received into them in payment of revenue, that have heretofore been made in pagodas, shall continue to be at the rate of 350. A: Rs. equivalent to 100 star pagodas.

"The Right Honorable the Governor in Council is pleased to declare his intention to prepare for circulation the fractional parts of the rupee, viz.:—Annas and pice, of which 16 annas are equal to one rupee, and 12 pice to one anna.

"For this purpose the new coinage of silver will consist of the silver rupee, the half rupee or 8-annas piece, and the quarter rupee or 4-annas piece, and the Right Honorable the Governor in Council is pleased to command that these shall circulate, and be received in payment at their established value.

"The Right Honorable the Governor in Council having abrogated the use of the gold star pagoda, has been pleased, for public convenience, to substitute the gold rupee, bearing the same inscription as the silver rupee, and of equal weight, viz., 180 grains, containing of fine gold 165 grains and alloy of silver 15 grains, which gold rupee will be issued and received in all payments of revenue at the rate of fifteen silver rupees for one gold rupee. . . . .

"The established and acknowledged circulating medium in specie of the Presidency of Fort St. George is hereby declared to be hereafter as follows:—

	Pure gold.	Alloy.	Total.
Gold rupee	Grs. 165	Grs. 15	Grs. 180
Half gold rupee	„ 82½	„ 7½	„ 90
Quarter „ „	„ 41¼	„ 3¾	„ 45
	Pure silver.		
Silver rupee	Grs. 165	„ 15	„ 180
„ half rupee	„ 82½	„ 7	„ 90
„ quarter „	„ 41¼	„ 3¾	„ 45
„ eighth „ or double anna ...	„ 20⅝	„ 1⅞	„ 22½
Single anna	„ $10\frac{5}{16}$	„ $\frac{15}{16}$	„ 11¼

"As it will not be practicable at once to recall from circulation the whole of the star pagodas and their fractional parts, the silver fanams and copper cash, the Right Honorable the Governor in Council is pleased to announce his resolution that they shall still continue to be received as often as they are tendered, in payment, until the whole can be withdrawn; that three rupees and a half shall be considered as representing the star pagoda, and that one star pagoda shall be equivalent to 45 fanams; that one rupee shall pass as heretofore for 12 fanams 68 cash, and 1 fanam for 80 cash.

"The copper coinage in circulation is also hereby declared to be continued until a sufficient quantity of copper pice can be prepared, adapted in weight to its relative value with the superior denomination of coin. . . . . . . its fractional parts."

It appears from the records that, in the course of the year 1817, an order was passed directing Collectors not to receive Pondicherry rupees in payment of revenue, but this order was rescinded on the receipt of a letter from the Collector of South Arcot to the effect that the old Pondicherry rupees, fanams, and cash had always been received into the district treasuries of that division, and that, if they were not received, it would tend much to impede the collections both in the Land and *Sayer* department; besides which it would fall very hard on the cultivators, for they would be obliged to pay a certain *vutum*, in order to get the village shroffs to exchange the Pondicherry coins for the Company's, and this would completely put the ryots at the mercy of the village bankers. It was accordingly resolved that the old Pondicherry rupee should be received in payment of revenue, so long as it continued to be distinguishable from the new one, specimens of which had been assayed, and found to manifest a striking variation both in their weight and fineness. The prohibition of the circulation of the Pondicherry rupee is referred to in a letter from the Collector of Salem regarding the receipt and payment of revenue in *Cantaroy* fanams, in reply to which it was stated in a letter, dated 24th February 1818, that "The Collector refers to the orders prohibiting the circulation of the Pondicherry rupee in the territories of the Hon'ble Company, and we are aware of no reason why a preference should be given the currency of the Mysore Government, particularly when the Hon'ble Company are at the great expense of mint establishments and recoinage. We would therefore recommend that the Collector of Salem be instructed not to receive in future Cantaroy fanams in payment of revenue, they being the coinage of the Mysore mint, which has issued so large a quantity of late, encouraged no doubt by the fallacious value given to them in the Hon'ble Company's territory, as to have proved a great source of inconvenience in the Ceded Districts. The same orders should be extended to the other Collectors in that quarter."

In the preamble of Regulation XIV, 1818, "for altering the 1818.
standard of the Calcutta sicca rupee [1] and gold mohur, and for further modifying some of the rules in force respecting these coins," it is stated that "the high standards established for the gold mohur and *sicca* rupee, having been found productive of many inconveniences, both to individuals and the public, inasmuch as they are ill-calculated to resist the wear and defacement to which coins are necessarily exposed, and as they are only to be obtained by having recourse to the expensive process of refining,

---

[1] Extract from a letter from the Assay Master, Fort St. George, dated 4th January 1821:—

"The people of these territories appear to call all coins which are issued by the Bengal Government *sicca* rupees; thus there are Cutke siccas, Nagapoor siccas, Jayapoor siccas, Bajeeron siccas, Narainpetta siccas, Benares, Farrukhábád, and others, but the Wallis rupees are understood to be the Calcutta sicca, the finest and heaviest of all."

diminishing consequently the productiveness of most of the sorts of bullion imported into the Company's territories; and it being desirable also that as much uniformity as can be established between the currencies circulating at the different presidencies should be introduced, consequently that an approximation of the Calcutta coins to the standard of those current at Madras and Bombay should be effected, it has been resolved to rescind the provisions of former regulations relative to the standard of the gold mohur and nineteenth sun *sicca* rupee, and to coin in future money of the proportions hereafter to be specified.

"As a reduction in the value of the sicca rupee, from its being in great measure the money of account, both in private and public transactions, would necessarily change the terms of all existing contracts, and might be productive of embarrassment and trouble, it has been determined to leave the rupee unaltered in this respect; and the new Calcutta *sicca* rupee will consequently contain the same quantity of fine silver as that heretofore struck; and, being of the same intrinsic value, will circulate on the same terms. The mint proportions of silver and gold being, it is believed, inaccurately estimated at present, and it being also desirable that an uniformity in this respect should be introduced at the three Presidencies of Calcutta, Madras and Bombay, it has been thought advisable to make a slight deduction in the intrinsic value of the gold mohur to be coined at this presidency, in order to raise the relative value of fine gold to fine silver, from the present rates of 1 to 14·861 to that of 1 to 15. The gold mohur will still continue to pass current at the present rate of sixteen rupees."

With respect to the new coinage at the Madras mint, which has already been referred to, two points for consideration remained after specimens of the gold coins had been minted, viz., whether they should be left plain or milled, and whether they should bear the date of the year in which they were minted. Specimens of the gold coins were forwarded to Government for approval, and a letter from the Secretary to Government to the Mint Committee, dated 26th January 1819, states that "The Right Honorable he Governor in Council concurs in your opinion that it is desirable to make a difference between the impressions of the gold and silver rupees, and also to alter the Persian inscription which those coins bear. The Governor in Council accordingly sanctions the specimens of gold coins submitted . . . . . ., except the English denominations under the Company's arms, which ought to be omitted. The Governor in Council desires that the coins may be milled, but not dated, as the shroffs might take advantage of the dates to impose a batta on the coinage of particular years." The draft of a proclamation on the proposed alteration of the impression of the gold coins, submitted to Government on the 9th of March 1819, stated that "The Right Honorable the Governor in Council has been pleased to resolve that the inscriptions on the gold rupee, the gold half rupee and the gold quarter rupee shall be different from those on the silver rupee, the silver half rupee, and the silver quarter rupee, and has accordingly directed that the gold rupee shall in future be impressed on the face with the Honorable Company's arms and the words

ENGLISH EAST INDIA COMPANY, and on the reverse with the words English Company's rupee in the Persian character; that the gold half rupee shall bear the Company's crest and the words ENGLISH EAST INDIA COMPANY on the face, and the words English Company's half rupee in the Persian character on the reverse; that the gold quarter rupee shall bear the Company's crest and the words ENGLISH EAST INDIA COMPANY on the face, and the words English Company's quarter rupee in the Persian character on the reverse.

By Regulation XI of 1819 the coinage of the Benares rupee was discontinued, and the Farrukhábád rupee declared the local currency of the province of Benares. "The Benares mint," Prinsep says:[1] "had been established by Rájá Balwant Singh in 1730. It remained under native management for twenty years after the province was ceded to the Company in 1775. The rupee had the full weight of one hundred and seventy-five grains, and was 2¼ per cent. better than the present rupee, or about equal to the Dihlí rupee of that date. It fell in value subsequently about four ánás per cent. and there, of course, remained under English management until it was abolished." 1819.

In a letter to Government, dated 8th March 1820, the Madras Mint Committee recommended that "the gold rupee should be divided into thirds instead of halves and quarters. The third would be of the value of five rupees, which is a most convenient sum for computation. A coin of that value, we have no doubt, would be in great request, and thus would both contribute to the convenience of the public, and, by promoting the circulation of gold, would maintain its relative value to the standard coin of the Government." The Mint Master was ordered to prepare a specimen of a *third*, to be submitted for the sanction of the Governor in Council. The main reason of the recommendation of the Mint Committee was that, as the gold rupee was equal in value to fifteen silver rupees, the half equal to seven rupees and a half, and the quarter to three rupees and three quarters, these fractional parts did not correspond to any exact number of the coins next inferior in denomination, and were of a value so inconvenient as to prevent their ever being much in use. 1820.

The following letter was addressed to Government by the Accountant-General, Fort St. George, on 28th February 1820:—

"By the report of the balance of the general treasury, dated the 20th instant, it is stated that there are no silver annas remaining, and, as it is expedient that there should be an ample supply of that coinage in substitution for the old and new Madras fanams which should be withdrawn from circulation, I beg to recommend that instructions be issued to the Mint Master to convert a greater portion of his silver balance into annas and to proceed upon the recoinage of the half and quarter pagoda, of dollar standard, including the five double and single fanam pieces.

"There is also in circulation a rupee of the coinage of 1807, of dollar standard, which should also be called in and recoined, as

[1] Op. cit., p. 26.

well as the new Arcot rupee, which is of British standard, or 11 ozs. 2 dwts.

"The old Arcot rupee is of a standard of superior fineness to the others, the recoinage of which may be a subject for consideration."

Directions were accordingly given to coin a sufficient number of double annas and quarter and half rupees, and then to recoin all the fanam pieces.

1821. The preamble of Regulation V, 1821, "for settling the rates at which Benares and Farrukhábád rupees shall be received in payment of the revenue of malguzars, whose engagements are expressed in Gohurshahee or Tirsolee rupees" states that "it is enacted by Regulation XI, 1819, that the Farrukhábád rupees shall be received within the province of Benares at par with the Benares rupees; but no provision has been made for regulating the exchange in account between the said rupees and the Gohurshahee and Tirsolee rupees, in which it appears that the engagements of many malguzars are expressed; moreover, the batta to be taken from such malguzars has hitherto been arbitrarily fixed, and considerable abuses have consequently prevailed. The intrinsic value of the coins having been now ascertained by a careful assay, whence it has appeared that the rupee denominated Chorah Gohurshahee exceeds, and the other descriptions of Gohurshahee equal the Farrukhábád rupee in value, and that the latter coin is 3-11-7 per cent. superior in value to the Tirsolee rupee, the Revenue officers have been directed to adjust their demands on the said malguzars according to the results of the assay, subject to the general principle of receiving the Farrukhábád rupee at par with the Benares rupee, and without any demand of batta on account of its inferiority in value below the local currency."

1823. It is stated in a letter from A. D. Campbell, Esq., Magistrate of Bellary, to the Madras Government, dated 27th April 1823, that a Brahmin, an inhabitant of Gudival in the Hyderabad territory, had tried to pass off 250 rupees of a suspicious nature, purporting to be of the Company's new coinage, in Kurnool, and stated, on examination, that they were forged by a goldsmith residing in the village of Muroor in the Hyderabad country. The Nabob was applied to, and detectives were sent to the goldsmith, who showed them all his utensils, and forged some coins in their presence. The practical suggestion was made by Mr. Campbell that the inscription on the Company's coin should be partly in English, in order to render the forgery of it more difficult, as, though the English soldiers would still continue to imitate the coin, natives would find it much more difficult to imitate exactly English characters than the native letters which were familiar to them. The further suggestion was made that a private mint mark might be placed on the coin, to be communicated to Collectors or their principal shroffs as a check upon forgery.

In 1823 a pice piece (fifty-three to the pound) with its half and quarter, were executed by W. Wyon for the East Indies, by the authority of the Secretary of State and the Master of the Mint. The obverse of these coins bore the arms of the Company and the motto AUSP. REGIS. & S. ANGLIAE, and the reverse a Persian inscription.[1]

The mint at Farrukhábád was abolished by Regulation II, 1824, it being considered no longer necessary to continue it, inasmuch as provision had been made by Regulation XXVI, 1817, for the coinage of the Farrukhábád rupee at any of the mints established by Government. 1824.

Early in 1824 specimens were prepared in the Madras mint of a rupee, which, while superior in workmanship to the current rupee, was stated to be also much better adapted for the currency of the Madras Presidency, and very difficult to counterfeit. It appears from a letter from the Registrar of the Zillah Court, Chingleput, to Government, dated 15th December 1823, that the most usual artifices by which coins were imitated or counterfeited at that time consisted in hollowing the centre of the old thick Company rupee, and filling up the cavity with lead, or striking off the impression from both sides of a thin Company rupee on copper, and covering the surface with about one-tenth of an inch of silver, and thereby making it only distinguishable from the original by its weight. But a still more lucrative speculation was carried on by gilding the silver rupee, which was of the same weight, and bore the same superscription as one species of the gold mohurs.

In the year 1825 the following correspondence took place with regard to the coinage of Prince of Wales' Island:— 1825.

From

THE SECRETARY TO GOVERNMENT,
Fort William,

To

THE SECRETARY TO GOVERNMENT,
Fort St. George.

SIR,

I am directed by the Right Honorable the Governor-General in Council to transmit to you the accompanying copy of correspondence relative to the supply of copper coinage required by the Penang Government, and to request that the Honorable the Governor in Council will be pleased to cause the coinage in question to be prepared at Fort St. George, if practicable, and transmitted to Penang.

2. Specimens of coins are herewith transmitted.

I have the honor to be,
Sir,
Your most obedient servant,

9th June 1825. HOLT MACKENZIE.

---

[1] Ruding, op. cit., vol. ii., p. 129.

From

THE ACTING SECRETARY TO GOVERNMENT,
Fort Cornwallis,

To

THE SECRETARY TO GOVERNMENT,
Fort St. William.

SIR,

The copper coin sent out by the Honorable Court of Directors, having been all issued from the treasury, and great inconvenience being likely to arise before a supply can be received from England, I am directed to forward specimens of the coins in use, the pice and half pice, in the hope that it may be found practicable to manufacture the same at the mint in Calcutta. These coins are issued, the first at 100, the second at 200 to the dollar, and pass at Singapore, and all over the Malay Peninsula, where they are much sought after. A coinage of a double pye, 50 to the dollar, bearing the same stamp, would also be convenient, should the measure be found practicable, and not attended with inconvenience. The transmission of the above coin to the amount of 10,000 dollars in value would prove extremely useful to the general condition of the island.

I have, &c., &c.,

9th April 1825. E. I. BLUNDELL.

The mint records show that, in consequence of this correspondence, new punches and dies were made, and 130,300 double pice, 136,700 single pice, and 145,000 half pice struck for the Penang Government.

As regards the earlier coinage of Pulo Pinang or Prince of Wales' Island, Marsden says: [1]

"There are in the collection a few specimens of small silver coins struck in Bengal for the use of the English settlement at this place. On one side is the customary mark of the East India Company, with the date 1788, and, on the other, in the Arabic character the barbarous words جزيرة پرنس ابويلس

"'Jezirah Prans ab Wailis,' for 'Prince of Wales' Island.' The weight of the large coin is 4 dwts. 4½ grs. and of the smaller, 1 dwt. 18 grs. There is also a small specimen in copper with the same inscription and date of 1787." Further Ruding figures [2] two coins bearing on the obverse the arms of the Company and the date 1810, and on the reverse the inscription 'Púlú Pinang,' surrounded by an ornamental border.

In a letter from the Bombay Government to the Secretary to Government, Fort St. George, dated Bombay Castle, 12th August 1824, it is stated that "The Honorable the Governor in Council has authorised those Bombay or Surat rupees termed Chapee, Soolakee, and Gabree rupees, which may be found in the consignments of treasure from Malabar, to be received at this presidency, the two first at a discount of 3 per cent. and the last at a discount

---

[1] Op. cit., p. 809, pl. liv, mcccxxviii.
[2] Op. cit., vol. ii, p. 405, pl. xvi, figs. 9, 10.

of 2 per cent. to cover the charges of recoinage." The meaning of the term 'Soolakee' has been already explained (p. 45) and the terms 'Chapee' and 'Gabree' are explained in a letter from the Collector of South Canara to the Accountant-General, Fort St. George, dated 26th March 1825, wherein it is stated that "The Chapee rupees are so called on account of their being impressed with a stamp, which they receive at the treasuries of the Native States where they have been circulated, and this stamp or chop does not in any way take away from their weight or value; on the contrary it may be considered an additional proof of their being genuine, as it is only after being shroffed in those treasuries that the mark is affixed by the treasurers.

"The Chapee-Soolakee has the additional mark of a nail, or other pointed instrument driven into the coin, to ascertain in the first instance that it is silver of the proper standard.

"The Gabree rupee is so called from the circumstance of a small piece of the metal having been rubbed or knocked off the coin in the course of circulation. It has its origin in general in the rupee being originally short of weight from the mould not being completely filled, when the rupee was struck, and a small portion of silver equal to the quantity deficient being subsequently added on the part imperfectly stamped. This piece of silver not being fused with the metal is liable to be rubbed off, and the coin from which it has been removed is called Gabree, and is more or less deficient in weight according to the size of the piece of silver that has been displaced and lost, which, however, is always very small, seldom exceeding the value of $\frac{3}{200}$ part of a rupee, or 1½ per cent."

The following correspondence bears on the currency at this 1829.
time in the Tenasserim Provinces:—

From

THE CIVIL COMMISSIONER,
Tenasserim Provinces,

To

THE CHIEF SECRETARY TO GOVERNMENT,
Fort William.

13*th January* 1829.

SIR,

A number of Madras pagodas and other coins, amounting in value to Madras rupees 19,328-13-0, having been collected in the treasuries at Tavoy and Mergui, and the common currency of these provinces being Madras rupees, I beg leave to transmit these coins, which the Burmese inhabitants are unwilling to receive, in order that the same may be sent to the mint at Calcutta and coined into rupees. I beg to enclose a list of the different coins and a receipt of the same.

I take this opportunity of soliciting that application may be made to the Government of Fort St. George to remit to me a supply of copper coinage to the extent in value of 20,000 Madras rupees for the use of these provinces in which the want of some suitable currency is very much felt.

I have, &c., &c.,

From

THE SECRETARY TO GOVERNMENT,
Fort William,

To

THE SECRETARY TO GOVERNMENT,
Fort St. George.

23rd January 1829.

SIR,

I am directed by the Governor-General in Council to transmit to you the accompanying copy of a letter from Mr. A. D. Maingy, Civil Commissioner for the Tenasserim Provinces, dated the 13th instant, and to request that the Right Honorable the Governor in Council will be pleased to order a supply of copper money to the extent of 20,000 Madras rupees to be consigned to that gentleman by the earliest convenient opportunity.

I have, &c., &c.,

1833. In 1833 a regulation (No. VII) was passed for altering the weight of the new Farrukhábád rupee, and for assimilating it to the legal currency of the Madras and Bombay Presidencies, for adjusting the weight of the Calcutta sicca rupee, and for fixing a standard limit of weight for India.

In the preamble of this regulation it is stated that "by a Resolution of the Governor-General in Council, dated the 10th of September 1824, the Farrukhábád rupee was ordered to be coined of one hundred and eighty grains, one hundred and sixty-five fine and fifteen alloy, and was declared the legal currency of the Saugor and Nerbuddah territories. It is considered expedient to adopt this weight and standard for the Farrukhábád rupee at the Calcutta as well as at the Saugor mint, instead of that described in section V, Regulation XI, 1819, from which it differs very slightly, and to make the Farrukhábád currency correspond in weight and intrinsic value with the new currency of the Madras and Bombay Presidencies. It is likewise convenient to make a trifling alteration in the weight of the Calcutta sicca rupee, as prescribed by clause 1, section 1, Regulation XIV, 1818. It is further convenient to introduce the weight of the Farrukhábád rupee as the unit of a general system of weights for Government transactions throughout India under the native and well-known denomination of the tola." [1]

---

[1] Note on tola. From Yule and Burnell, op. cit.

"Tola, s., an Indian weight (chiefly of gold or silver) not of extreme antiquity. Hind. *tola* (Sansk. tuta, a balance, *tul* to lift up, to weigh). The Hindu scale is 8 *rattis* = 1 másha, 12 *máshas* = 1 *tola*. Thus the *tola* was equal to 96 *rattis*.

1563. "I knew a Secretary of Nizamoxa, a native of Coracon, who ate every day three *tollas* of opium, which is the weight of ten cruzados and a half."

1610. "A *tola* is a rupee *challany* of silver, and ten of these *toles* are the value of one of gold." *Hawkins*, in *Purchas*, 1, 217.

1615-16. "Two *tole* and a half being an ounce." *Sir T. Roe*, in *Purchas*, 1, 545.

In section ii of the same regulation it is stated that " the use of the sicca weight of 179·666, hitherto employed for the receipt of bullion at the mint, being in fact the weight of the Moorshedabad rupee of the old standard, which was assumed as the sicca currency of the Honorable Company's Provinces of Bengal, Behar and Orissa, shall be discontinued, and in its place the following unit, to be called the tola, shall be introduced, which, from its immediate connection with the rupee of the Upper Provinces and of Madras and Bombay, will easily and speedily become universal through the British territories.

" The tola or sicca weight to be equal to one hundred and eighty grains troy, and the other denominations of weight to be derived from this unit, according to the following scale, viz. :—

8 rattis = 1 masha = 15 troy grains.
12 mashas = 1 tola = 180 troy grains.
80 tolas (sicca weight) = 1 seer = 2½ lbs. troy.
40 seers = 1 mun, or bazar maund = 100 lbs. troy."

This system of weights was ordered to be adopted at the Mints and Assay Offices of Calcutta and Saugor, respectively, in the adjustment and verification of all weights for Government or public purposes, sent thither for examination.

The Mysore mint, which was abolished in 1843, was removed from Mysore to Bangalore in 1833, in which year it appears from the following letter to the Madras Government to have been the intention to have the copper coinage supplied by the Madras mint.

COMMISSIONER'S OFFICE,

Bangalore, 23*rd August* 1833.

SIR,

I am directed by the Commissioners for the affairs of Mysore to . . . . explain that, in making the application contained in my letter of the 20th June last, the Commissioners acted under an impression that an ample stock of copper coin received from Europe might probably be in store at Madras, and disposable for the use of Mysore.

As this however is not the case, and as the Commissioners find that they can have the coin made at Bangalore (a course of proceeding which does not appear to them liable to any serious objection) on more advantageous terms than those on which it could be supplied from Madras, they direct me to state that it is not their intention to avail themselves of the offer, which the Right Honorable the Governor in Council has had the goodness to make to them of the Madras mint on this occasion.

I have, &c., &c.,

In 1833 the abolition of the Madras mint was recommended by the Calcutta Mint Committee, and the following extract from a letter, dated 29th January 1834, shows the feeling of the Court of Directors on this subject :—

"The grounds upon which the Calcutta Mint Committee have come to the conclusion that the Madras mint may be abolished without injury to the public interests are as follows: It appears from their report that since 1882-83 the annual average importation of bullion into the territories of your Government by sea has been about 44 lakhs, while the average annual export has amounted to 63 lakhs, showing an excess of export by sea to the amount of 19 lakhs. From this fact they are led to conclude that the local currency, as far as required for domestic purposes, has not been derived from foreign bullion. They next proceed to inquire whether any large source of supply is furnished to your mint by the inland trade, and they state that the average import of bullion from the interior does not much exceed 4 lakhs of rupees a year, so that, unless the receipts from the Government revenue itself afford the materials of the coinage which takes place in the mint, very little of the business carried on there can arise from the coinage necessary to meet the internal demands of the Madras territories. The recoinage from the Government revenue they consider must be very small, as even in the Calcutta mint it does not amount to 3½ lakhs of rupees a year on an average.

"The average amount of the coinage at the Madras mint from 1815 to 1820 was 50 lakhs a year, and, from 1817 to 1828, 68 lakhs, but during the latter part of the period, viz., from May 1825 to May 1828 it was only 42 lakhs.

"The net annual export of bullion from Madras, it has been seen, is 19 lakhs of rupees, and as there are no mines in the country and the import from the interior in the course of trade is only 4 lakhs a year, the immediate inference would be that nearly the whole of the net export of 19 lakhs must have been made in the current coin of the country. But it appears in fact to have been even much larger. The Calcutta Mint Committee state that the average annual export of silver coin, intending, it is to be presumed, Madras rupees, for the last 4 years has been nearly 50 lakhs; consequently the bullion imported has been re-exported in the shape of coin, and the mint has been employed very unnecessarily in charging its . . . . . at a gratuitous wastage and expense. The Committee then observe that the export of coin from Madras was chiefly on public account. In 1824-25 and 1825-26 large sums were sent to Ava for the purpose of paying the Madras troops employed in the war, and a large supply goes also annually to Bombay, which, now that an effective mint has been established at that presidency, might as well be sent in the shape of bullion. The average amount of coinage required for domestic circulation under the Madras Presidency will therefore, it is said, not be more than 10 or 15 lakhs a year, which, if it were coined at the Calcutta mint and forwarded thence to Madras, would render it practicable to effect an annual saving, by abolishing the Madras mint, to the extent of at least 60,000 rupees a year.

"We have carefully considered the facts and reasonings brought forward by the Calcutta Mint Committee upon this subject, and we think that the conclusion to which they have come is a just one. We cannot indeed admit the propriety of their statement that the Madras mint 'has been employed very unnecessarily in changing the form of the bullion imported at a gratuitous wastage and expense,' because it is evident that the conversion of that bullion into coin was required for important public purposes; but it seems quite clear that this coinage may for the future be conducted at the Calcutta and Bombay mints without leading to any material inconvenience, and at a great saving of expense to the State. Such an arrangement has become still more desirable than ever from this circumstance, of which you probably are aware, that the machinery of the new Calcutta and Bombay mints (the erection of which has occasioned such a large outlay of money) was fabricated upon a scale sufficient to enable those two mints combined to supply the whole of the coinage necessary for British India, and the present coinage at the new Calcutta mint is not by any means so extensive as to employ the powers of which the machinery is capable. In addition to the facts stated by the Calcutta mint as above referred to, we observe by a more recent account received from you that the value of the coinage in your mint, which had fallen in the years 1825—1828 to an average of 42 lakhs of rupees, was in 1828-29 not quite 27 lakhs, and in 1829-30 was little more than 22 lakhs."

In obedience to the orders of Government, in consequence of this letter, the Madras Mint Committee called on the mercantile community, both European and Native, requesting the former to state "whether, in the event of the accommodation which the mint has heretofore afforded being withdrawn, it would, in their opinion, affect the commercial interest of the Madras Presidency, and, if so, in what manner and to what extent. The native merchants were requested to state whether they thought the abolition of the mint would injure the trade of the port, and in what manner and to what extent." The concurrent opinion of the entire mercantile community, with the exception of Messrs. Parry, Dare and Co., was that very serious injury would be done to the commercial interests of the presidency by abolishing the mint, and the Mint Committee came to the conclusion that "the existence of the mint is essential to the interests of the public; that its continuance is inseparably connected with the prosperity of this settlement, and necessary to the due administration of its finances; and, should it be abolished, and Government should find it expedient to re-establish it, such a measure would be attended with much expense and difficulty, arising from the dispersion of the present establishment and the impracticability hereafter to collect them again in the public service, or to find properly qualified persons to supply their place."

In 1834 pattern rupees were struck, bearing the following 1834.
devices and legends:—

1. *Obverse.*—Bust of the King (William IV) r, and legend GULIELMUS. IIII. D.G. BRITT. ET. IND. REX. surrounded by a wavy line.

Reverse.—In the centre ONE RUPEE with lotus flower above, and date 1834 below, surrounded by a wreath; around EAST INDIA COMPANY, and the value in Persian, Nágarí, and Bengálí.

(pl. xx-7.)

2. Similar to No. 1, except the legend on the obveres GULIELMUS. IIII. D.G. BRITANNIAR. REX. F.D.

3. Similar to No. 2, but thicker and smaller.

4. Similar to No. 1, except the legend on the obverse WILLIAM. IV. KING.

5. *Obverse.*—Similar to No. 4.

Reverse.—A lion and palm tree and the legend BRITISH INDIA.

6. *Obverse.*—A lion and palm tree, and the legend BRITISH INDIA.

Reverse.—In the centre ONE RUPEE with lotus flower above, and date 1834 below, surrounded by a wreath; around EAST INDIA COMPANY, and the value in Persian, Nágarí, and Bengálí.

1835. On March 31st, 1835, a letter was addressed to the Governor-General by the Calcutta Mint Committee relative to the promulgation of a new uniform coinage for British India, in which it is stated that: "We have now the honor to submit specimens of a rupee bearing the device of Flaxman's lion, selected by Lord William Bentinck as in his lordship's opinion the best adopted for the coin of British India.

"2. The Mint Master explains in his letter accompanying these specimens, that, in consequence of their being struck from the matrix die and not in the regular coinage presses, they are defective on the edge for want of the collar.

"3. Mr. Saunders has also at our request furnished specimens of the King's head rupee, in order that your Honor in Council may judge of the two together. One of the latter specimens has the straight milling of the English coin, which we are inclined to prefer to the plain edge.

"4. The opinion we formerly ventured to express in favor of the device of His Majesty's head is by no means lessened by the present comparison. An emblematical design, however appropriate it may be for the *reverse* of a handsome medal or medallic coin, such as we would make of the gold mohur, seems to us by no means so well suited for the *obverse* of the current coins as the effigy of the reigning monarch, and in regard to the danger of forgery there can be no doubt that a correct drawing of the human head, which all the world is in the constant habit of observing so as to tell at a glance the slightest difference of feature, is both easier to recognise and more difficult to imitate than the contour of an animal seldom or never seen by the majority of mankind. This argument cannot be better illustrated than by the fact that the lion was engraved in twenty-six days, while the head occupied upwards of one month and ten days.

"5. We beg leave to submit an impression in pure gold of the King's head with the lion as a reverse, proposed as a double gold mohur of 360 grains standard.

"6. Captain Forbes has submitted a memorandum on the expediency of requesting the Honorable Court of Directors to procure well-executed matrix dies of such devices as may finally be adopted from Mr. Wyon, the Chief Engraver of the London Mint.

" 7. This would doubtless be an excellent guide for our native engravers, but we do not think it necessary to suspend the introduction of the new device until it is obtained, the present matrices being in our opinion quite good enough for the purpose.

" 8. It would be highly desirable, however, to procure a good collection of modern medals and coins from England to serve as models for our native school of die engravers, and it will be particularly requisite to be furnished from the London mint with proof impressions of the King's head, especially on the occasion of a new sovereign. The present head is copied from an English gold coin procured in the bazar, and considerably rubbed on the surface.

" 9. It may be satisfactory to inform your Honor in Council that we have ascertained from Colonel Presgrave, Mint and Assay Master at Saugor, that he will be able to strike the new coin in his mint, if provided with collar dies instead of those now furnished to him.

" 10. There is then no obstacle to the introduction at once of the new currency, if only reasonable time be allowed for the preparation or multiplication of dies (of which unfortunately the supply on hand is small). The coinage of *sicca* rupees has been for some time suspended as a preliminary measure.

" 11. With reference to this last point and to the adoption of the 180 grain rupee as the universal coin of British India, we beg leave to call the attention of your Honor in Council to the expediency of changing at the same time the rupee of account in the general books of this presidency.

" 12. The maintaining of the sicca rupee in account after its coinage has been abolished would be evidently impolitic, and even now, from the erroneous valuation given to the Farrukhábád rupee in exchange ($104\frac{1}{8}$ to 100 siccas), considerable inconvenience is experienced in adjusting accounts between the Mint and the Accountant-General's offices, and the Collectors of the upper provinces. Should the new unit be adopted, it will be advisable to convert all *sicca* values and amounts into it at the intrinsic par of $\frac{16}{15}$ to avoid the confusion of the fictitious exchange hitherto employed."

In reply to this letter the Secretary to Government was ordered to inform the Mint Committee that:

" 1. The rupee having on one side the device of His Majesty's head, and on the reverse the inscription EAST INDIA COMPANY, together with the nominal value of the coin in English, Persian and Nágarí, and the representation of a lotus flower and myrtle wreath, has been approved by the Governor-General in Council as the model for the future coinage of the rupee of British India. Your suggestion for introducing on this coin the straight milling of the English currency is also approved and sanctioned.

" 2. The Governor-General in Council does not contemplate suspending the introduction of the new device until matrix dies can be obtained from England. You will be therefore pleased to communicate with the Madras, Bombay and Saugor mints, with the view of effecting a change in the rupee currency throughout British India with all convenient expedition.

"3. It will be, of course, necessary as subservient to the measure to change the rupee of account on the general books of this presidency as suggested by you. The Governor-General in Council, on the adoption of the new unit, approves of the conversion of all *sicca* value and amounts into it at the intrinsic par of $\frac{16}{15}$.

"4. I am directed to call for further reports and suggestions from you as to a corresponding change in the gold and copper currency of British India, which it will be advisable to submit at your earliest convenience."

In a further letter from Government, the Mint Committee of Calcutta was informed that "It has this day (22nd April 1835) resolved to inscribe on the reverse of the new silver coinage the denomination of value in the English and Persian languages only, and to have no difference whatever in the dies of the several presidencies. The year (1835) of the die will represent the era of the alteration of the coins, and will not need to be changed until a new coin shall be ordered to be struck. On the face of the coin with His Majesty's head it will be sufficient to stamp the name of the Sovereign WILLIAM IV, without the word *King*." But in a further letter, dated 13th May 1835, it is stated that "the selection of the Governor-General in Council has fallen upon the specimen with the inscription WILLIAM IV KING, as none of the others without the word *King* are approved. The above legend is accordingly to be adopted for the obverse of the new coin."

The details of the new coinage were finally laid down by Act XVII, 1835, wherein it was enacted "that from the 1st day of September 1835, the undermentioned silver coins *only* shall be coined at the mints within the territories of the East India Company; a rupee to be denominated the Company's rupee; a half rupee, a quarter rupee, and a double rupee; and the weight of the said rupee shall be 180 grains troy, and the standard shall be as follows:—

$\frac{11}{12}$ or 165 grains of pure silver;
$\frac{1}{12}$ or 15 grains of alloy;

and the other coins shall be of proportionate weight and of the same standard.

"And that these coins shall bear on the obverse the head and the name of the *reigning* sovereign of the United Kingdom of Great Britain and Ireland, and on the reverse the designation of the coin in English and Persian, and the words EAST INDIA COMPANY in English with such embellishment as shall from time to time be ordered by the Governor-General in Council.

"And that the Company's rupee, half rupee, and double rupee shall be a legal tender in satisfaction of all engagements, provided the coin shall not have lost more than 2 per cent. in weight, and provided it shall not have been clipped or filed, or have been defaced otherwise than by use.

"And that the said rupee shall be received as equivalent to the Bombay, Madras, Farrukhábád and Sonat rupees, and to fifteen-sixteenths of the Calcutta sicca rupee; and the half and double rupee respectively shall be received as equivalent to the half and double of the abovementioned Bombay, Madras, Farrukhábád and Sonat rupees, and to the half and double of fifteen-sixteenths of the Calcutta sicca rupee . . . .

"And that the undermentioned gold coins only shall henceforth be coined at the mints within the territories of the East India Company :—

First, a gold mohur of 15 rupee-piece, of the weight of 180 grains troy, and of the following standard, viz. :—

$\frac{11}{12}$ or 165 grains of pure gold.
$\frac{1}{12}$ or 15 grains of alloy.

Second, a five-rupee piece equal to a third of a gold mohur.

Third, a ten-rupee piece equal to two-thirds of a gold mohur.

Fourth, a thirty-rupee piece, or double gold mohur.

"And the three last-mentioned coins shall be of the same standard with the gold mohur, and of proportionate weight.

"And that these gold coins shall bear on the obverse the head and name of the reigning sovereign of the United Kingdom of Great Britain and Ireland, and on the reverse the designation of the coin in English and Persian, and the words EAST INDIA COMPANY in English, with such embellishment as shall from time to time be ordered by the Governor-General in Council, which shall always be different from that of the silver coinage.

"And that no gold coin shall henceforward be a legal tender of payment in any of the territories of the East India Company.

"And that it shall be competent to the Governor-General in Council, in his executive capacity, to direct the coining and issuing of all coins authorised by this Act; to prescribe the devices and inscriptions of the copper coins issued from the mints in the said territories, and to establish, regulate, and abolish mints, any law hitherto in force to the contrary notwithstanding."

In the same year (1835) an Act (No. XXI) was passed, by which it was enacted "that from the 20th day of December 1835 the following copper coins only shall be issued from any mint within the Presidency of Bengal :—

1. A pice weighing .. .. .. 100 grs. troy,
2. A double pice weighing .. .. 200 ,,
3. A pice, or one-twelfth of an anna weighing .. .. .. $33\frac{1}{3}$,,

with such devices as shall be fixed for the same by the Governor-General in Council."

By the same Act it was further enacted "that from the said 20th of December 1835, the said pice shall be legal tender for $\frac{1}{64}$ of the Company's rupee, and the said double pice for $\frac{1}{32}$ of the Company's rupee and the said pie for $\frac{1}{192}$ of the Company's rupee. Provided always that, after the said 20th of December 1835, no copper coin shall in any part of the territories of the East India Company be legal tender, except for fractions of a rupee."

In the following year (1836) it was enacted by Act XIII, that "from the 1st January 1838, the Calcutta sicca rupee shall cease to be a legal tender in discharge of any debt, but shall be received by the Collectors of land revenue, and at all other treasuries, by weight, and subject to a charge of 1 per cent. for recoinage. 1836.

"And that from the 1st of June 1836, Section V, Regulation XXV, 1817, of the Bengal Code that the pice struck at the mints of Benares and Farrukhábád agreeably to the provisions of Regulation X, 1809, and Regulation VII, 1814, and Regulation XXI, 1816, shall be considered as circulating equally with the pice of Calcutta coinage throughout the provinces of Bengal, Behar and in Orissa, and shall in like manner be received as a legal tender in payment of the fractional parts of a rupee of the local currency at the rate of sixty-four pice for each rupee, shall be repealed; and the said pice shall be a legal tender only within the provinces and places for which they were respectively coined....."

In a letter from the Government of India to the Madras Mint Committee, dated 17th December 1836, in which the question, whether the Madras mint should be restored temporarily or permanently and for the coinage of what metal, is discussed at great length, it is stated that "the coinage of silver having been shewn not to be necessary on the one hand and of doubtful practicability on the other, the only question that remains respects the copper coinage of the Madras Presidency, the supply of which is stated to be deficient in the extreme. The coinage of copper has been suspended in the Calcutta mint for two reasons—*first*, because of the urgent demand for silver in replacement of the sicca currency of Bengal, and *secondly*, because the price of copper has risen so much beyond previous averages, that the coinage ceased to yield the same profit as heretofore .... The mint of Calcutta having an excess of power available, and the expectation of ability to purchase copper on reasonable terms, the question recurs, whether this coinage shall be prosecuted for replacement of the existing copper currency of Bengal and the North-West Provinces, or part of the coinage shall be diverted to supply the wants of Madras.

"The determination of this question must rest on the decision that may be come to in respect to the expediency and possibility of continuing in circulation the old pyce, which the Government have latterly restored to credit. If this currency be not recalled and displaced, a small addition to the existing currency is all that can be required to keep the copper circulation steady at its legal tender par. But, if the copper currency of Bengal is to be entirely renovated, there will be no spare power in the mint to give to the striking of copper for Madras.

"The Right Honorable the Governor-General of India in Council is inclined at present to the opinion that it will be necessary eventually to call in and replace the old pyce of the former Calcutta mint. On this account, therefore, as well as on the ground that the coinage of copper can be commenced at Madras at a small cost and without delay, Rs. 2,000 only being required to set up the machinery and an establishment to work it, and because also there will be no difficulty or loss hereafter in stopping such a coinage, when it shall be no longer required, His Lordship in Council sanctions the proposition of Mr. Braddock that this coinage shall immediately be undertaken with the means available, provided the copper can be purchased at the price stated as that of tenders made to this mint, viz., Rs. 42 per Indian mun[1] or 100 lbs. troy, or, if the metal can be furnished from the Government stores."

From 1837 till 1840, during which time the mint machinery was undergoing repairs, the Madras records are silent; but it appears from a letter from the Mint Master, dated 17th February 1840, that the repairs were at that time so far advanced as to render it necessary that the preparation of the dies for the ensuing coinage should be commenced as soon as possible, so that the coinage might be proceeded with as soon as possible. It was about the same time pointed out that new Company's silver rupees, half, and quarter rupees, were the coins which it would be most desirable to strike off on the first opening of the mint, simultaneously with copper single pie pieces.

In a letter from the Calcutta Mint Committee, dated 14th December 1839, it is stated that "Captain Smith in his report to the Madras Government having impugned the artistical execution of the coinage of this mint, so far as concerns the device of the Company's rupee hitherto coined, in the accuracy of which we, as well as the Mint Master, entirely agree, the Mint Master has reminded us that, in the original communications to the Honorable Court in 1819, the necessity for a properly-qualified die engraver was strongly pointed out to the Honorable Court, and that the appointment of an engraver, consequent upon that representation, was then not made only because the mint was not sufficiently advanced to require his services. We think it our duty to state that we have had every reason to be satisfied with our present engraver, of whose efforts to produce an effigy of Her present Majesty from a sovereign we have the honor to forward a specimen; but, as he is at present the only competent engraver available, and has resisted every solicitation of the officers of the mint to instruct others in his art who might take up his duty when he was unwell or eventually succeed him, we are bound in duty to declare our conviction that it has become absolutely necessary that an able engraver should be sent out by the Honorable Court to take upon him, jointly with Kasheenauth, the duty of die engraver, and of preparing plates of steel or copper as the Mint Master and the Accountant-General for the time being shall direct, and to instruct such persons in the art of engraving to be his assistants and successors, as the Mint Committee for the time being shall direct to be placed under his instructions for these purposes." 1839.

By proclamation, dated November 18th, 1840, the Governor-General in Council was pleased to notify that "from and after the 1840.

---

[1] Note from Yule and Burnell, op. cit.

"The values of the *man* as a weight, even in modern times, have varied immensely, *i.e.*, from little more than 2 lbs. to upwards of 160. The 'Indian maund' which is the standard of weight in British India, is of 40 *sers*, each *ser* being divided into 16 chitaks; and this is the general scale of sub-division in the local weights of Bengal and Upper and Central India, though the value of the *ser* varies. That of the standard *ser* is 80 *tolas* or rupee-weights and thus the *maund* = 82⅞ lbs. avoirdupois. The Bombay maund (*or man*) of 40 *sers* = 28 lbs.; the Madras one of 40 *sers* = 25 lbs. The Palloda *man* of Ahmadnagar contained 64 *sers*, and was = 163¼ lbs. This is the largest *man* we find in 'the Useful Tables.' The smallest Indian *man* again is that of Colachy in Travancore and = 18 lbs. 12 oz. 13 drs."

11th day of November 1840 in respect to the mint of Calcutta, and from and after the 1st day of April 1841 in respect to the mint of Fort St. George and Bombay, those parts of Act XVII of 1835 which were suspended by Act XXXI of 1837 (on the accession of Queen Victoria), directing that certain silver coins issued from the mints within the territories of the East India Company shall bear on the obverse the head of the reigning sovereign of the United Kingdom of Great Britain and Ireland, will be again in force; and that the device of the silver coins which shall be coined from and after the said dates, respectively, in the mints of India, in conformity with Acts XVII of 1835 and XXI of 1838, will be as Act XVII of 1835 enacts, viz.:—

On the *obverse* the head of Her Majesty Victoria with the words VICTORIA QUEEN.

On the *reverse* the denomination of the coin in English and Persian in the centre encircled by a wreath and around the margin the words EAST INDIA COMPANY, 1840.

"The coin will be milled on the edge with a serrated or upright milling, like the rupee now current bearing the head of his late Majesty William IV.

"The weight, standard, fineness and value of the Company's rupees as defined in the Act are here repeated. Weight, 180 grains troy, or one tolah. Standard quality eleven-twelfths silver one-twelfth alloy value. The same as the Company's rupee of 1835, the Madras, Bombay, Farrukhábád and Sonat rupee, and equal to fifteen-sixteenths of the late sicca rupee.

"The other silver coins authorised to be issued from the Government mint by Act XVII of 1835, and Act XXI of 1838, viz.: —double, half, and quarter rupees, and two-anna pieces will bear in all respects a due proportion to this rupee."

1841. By a further proclamation, dated February 10th, 1841, the Governor-General in Council was pleased to notify "that the gold coins henceforth to be issued from the Government mints at the different presidencies in India in conformity with Act XVII of 1835 shall bear the following device:—

"On the *obverse* the head of Her Majesty Queen Victoria with the words VICTORIA QUEEN, 1841.

"On the *reverse* a lion and a palm tree in the centre, with the designation of the coin in English and Persian below, and around the margin the words EAST INDIA COMPANY.

"The coin will be milled on the edge like the rupee. The weight and standard will be according to the Act as follows: Weight of the gold mohur or fifteen-rupee piece, 180 grs. troy; standard of ditto, $\frac{11}{12}$ or 165 grs. pure gold, $\frac{1}{12}$ or 15 grs. alloy.

"The other gold coins, viz., the five-rupee, ten-rupee, and thirty-rupee or double gold mohur pieces, will be of the same standard as the gold mohur or fifteen-rupee piece, and of proportionate weight."

1843. In a letter, dated 7th April 1843, the Assay Master to the Madras Mint wrote to the effect that he once proposed to Lord William Bentinck, when Governor-General, a spelter or zinc coinage of money which, as the method of rendering that metal malleable had become generally known, might have been effected at a small expense, and been made with considerable profit to the Company, superseded the use of cowrie shells, and most likely been melted down to form brass, as the copper was in various parts of the Company's dominions, thus affording a continued source of profit to the Company.

By Act XIII, 1844, it was enacted "that, from the 1st day of August 1844, the Trisoolee pice struck for the province of Benares, under the provisions of Regulations X of 1809 and VII of 1814, and at the Saugor mint, shall cease to be a legal tender within the province of Benares. 1844.

"And that until the said 1st day of August 1844, such Trisoolee pice shall be received on account of the Government, and shall be exchanged by take (that is to say, every Trisoolee pice paid in shall be received as one Company's pice and one Company's pice shall be given for every Trisoolee pice presented for exchange) at such treasuries or other places within the province of Benares as shall be pointed out for that purpose in any proclamation of the Lieutenant-Governor of the North-Western Provinces. . . . .

"And that it shall be lawful for the said Lieutenant-Governor, if he shall see fit, to order that in any case one Company's rupee shall be given for every sixty-four Trisoolee pice so presented for exchange, and that in every case one Company's rupee shall be given for every sixty-four Trisoolee pice accordingly."

In 1844 a further Act (No. XXII) was passed "for regulating the copper coinage of the mints in the territories of the East India Company," by which it was enacted "that from and after the passing of this Act the following copper coins only shall be issued from any mint within the territories of the East India Company :—

1. A pice weighing	100	grs. troy.
2. Double pice weighing	200	"
3. A pie or one-twelfth of an anna weighing	$33\frac{1}{3}$	"

with such devices as shall be fixed for the same by the Governor-General in Council.

"And that from and after the passing of this Act the said pice shall be a legal tender throughout the territories of the East India Company for $\frac{1}{64}$ of the Company's rupee, and the said double pice for $\frac{1}{32}$ of the Company's rupee, and the said pie for $\frac{1}{192}$ of the Company's rupee."

In a minute by a member of the Madras Mint Committee on the question of the advisability of the practice of receiving uncurrent coins at the provincial treasuries, dated 1st April 1845, it is stated that "the practice of receiving uncurrent coins at the provincial treasuries at certain rates of exchange has existed almost from the period of the assumption of the country, and was adopted mainly, if not entirely, with the view of displacing the old currency by the new. . . . It would be desirable to ask the opinion of the Board of Revenue whether they considered the refusal generally in all districts to receive a foreign currency at the provincial treasuries in payment of revenue would be attended with any prejudicial effects; if not, I should make the refusal a general one. I would propose, however, that the prohibition should 1845.

be confined to the currency of native states and foreign European. The old Arcot rupees and all former coins issued from the Company's mints, including star pagodas and the Company's former rupees, as well as Bombay and sicca rupees, should continue to be received as hitherto. The Bombay-Soorat rupee, in which coin a considerable portion of the land revenue of the Bellary district is paid, is now classed, and I think improperly so, as uncurrent coin, and these should continue to be received at par, as they have hitherto been. We should under this system avoid all the evils attendant on the iniquitous practice adopted by Native Governments of debasing their coin from time to time, while all coins which have been issued from provinces now forming an integral portion of the British territory in India will continue to be received, till they wholly disappear from circulation.

"I would except, however, one coin from the general rule, namely, Spanish dollars. The rate of conversion at which they are received yields a large profit on recoinage. They are likely to be in demand at any time for remittance to China or on Eastern settlements, and they are by far the best form of bullion to send to England, if the Home treasury should be in need of specie remittances from this country. I think in 1838-1839 the Court of Directors particularly desired to have Spanish dollars in such cases."

In the same year a proposal was before the Madras Mint Committee as to the coinage of silver single anna pieces for the Ceylon Government.

1851. In March 1851 a proposal was made by the Assay Master, Fort St. George, that, in consequence of the general complaint of the want of currency suited to the exigencies of the lower orders throughout the territories of the East India Company, a zinc, or as it was commercially termed spelter coinage, representing the hundredth part of an anna, should be established, which would afford a profit equal to that of copper coinage, and would, it was thought, in time, supersede the use of cowries, the value of which fluctuated to the detriment of the vast multitude among whom it was current. It was also proposed that a trifling alteration might be made with regard to the copper coinage, a piece of the value of the tenth of an anna being substituted for the pie, and one of the value of the fifth of an anna for the three-pie pieces. But, as the abolition of the Madras mint was at that time under consideration, the proposals were not entertained.

A letter from the Mint Master, Calcutta, to the Mint Master, Madras, dated 30th June 1851, states that "in continuation of my letter intimating the dispatch of two matrices and six punches for the Queen Victoria rupee, I have now the honour to intimate that I have this day forwarded to the General Post Office for dispatch to you one box containing three obverse and three reverse punches for the Queen Victoria half rupee, as also three obverse and three reverse punches for the Queen Victoria quarter rupee.

"The obverse of the rupee punches last supplied and of the half rupee punches now forwarded have been obtained from original matrices engraved by Mr. Wyon of the Royal Mint, London, and transmitted to Calcutta by the Honorable the Court of Directors. The punches for the reverse have, however, been struck from matrices engraved by the Calcutta mint engraver, but are the same in design as those executed by Mr. Wyon, only having such a slight convexity as was found requisite to enable the dies formed by them to bring up the impressions on the coins.

"The punches for the quarter rupee have been obtained from the original English matrix, and they will therefore require to have the last two figures of the year (40) sunk in the die after it has been multiplied.

"The dies now in use in the mint for the whole, the half, and the quarter Victoria rupee bear date 1840, as has been considered desirable, to prevent the shroffs from charging a discount on the coins bearing this date, as they would do if the coins now issuing bore the date of the present year.

"Punches for the eight-rupee or the two-anna silver piece will be ready for dispatch by the next steamer."

In Notification, No. 26, dated Fort William, 22nd December 1852.
1852, it is stated that "by section 9, Act XVII of 1835, of the Government of India, it was enacted, that thenceforward no gold coin should be a legal tender of payment in any of the territories of the East India Company; and, accordingly, gold ceased from the date of the passing of the Act to be a legal tender of payment in the Company's territories in India.

"But, by a proclamation issued on the 13th January 1841, officers in charge of public treasuries were authorized freely to receive gold coins, struck in conformity with the provisions of the same Act XVII of 1835, at the rates indicated by the denomination of the pieces, until they should have passed certain limits of lightness, set forth in a table published with the proclamation, or until further orders; and gold coins have been thus received in liquidation of public demands up to the present date.

"Notice is now given . . . . . that on and after that date (1st January 1853), no gold coin will be received on account of payments due, or in any way to be made to the Government . . . . Gold will continue as heretofore to be received into any of the mints . . . . for coinage, under the Act and rules at present in force for the coinage of gold, but mint certificates for gold coins will be discharged in gold only, and no such certificate for gold will be accepted in any public treasury in liquidation of public demands, or on account of any payment to the Government whatever."

In 1854 an Act was passed "to amend Act No. XXI of 1853 1854.
and Act No. XXII of 1844, and to authorise the issue of half pice," by which it was enacted that "after the passing of this Act, copper coins to be called half pice may be issued from any of the mints in the territories under the Government of the East India Company.

"A half pice shall weigh fifty grains troy, and shall be a legal tender in any part of the said territories for $\frac{1}{128}$th part of the Company's rupee, but shall not be a legal tender, except for fractions of a rupee."

Repealed by Act No. XIII, 1862.

1858. The charter of the Company was renewed for the last time in 1853, only, however, for so long as Parliament should ordain, and the number of Directors was reduced, and their patronage as regards appointments to the Civil Service was taken away, so as to make way for the principle of open competition. Five years later, on the 1st November 1858, at a durbar held at Allahabad, the royal proclamation was sent forth, which announced that Queen Victoria had assumed the Government of India, and so the career of the East India Company terminated after an existence of more than two-and-a-half centuries.

1862. So much of Act XVII, 1835, as provided that only the silver coins therein mentioned shall be coined, &c., and that they shall bear the words EAST INDIA COMPANY; also Act XXXI, 1837; Act XXII, 1844; and Act XI, 1854, except as to coin already issued, were repealed by Act No. XIII of 1862, by which it was enacted as follows:—

I. From the first day of November 1862, so much of the 1st and 2nd sections of Act XVII of 1835 (*relating to gold and silver coinage*), as provides that only the silver coins therein mentioned shall be coined at the mints within the territories of the East India Company, and that such coins shall bear on the reverse the words EAST INDIA COMPANY; also Act XXXI of 1837 (*relating to coinage*), Act XXI of 1838 (*relating to the silver coin*), Act XXII of 1844, and Act XI of 1854 (*relating to the copper coin*), shall be repealed, except as to any Act already done, or coin already coined or issued under the same.

II. From the first day of November 1862, except as provided by Act XVI of 1847 (*for establishing a copper currency in the Settlements of Penang, Singapore and Malacca*), in respect of cents, half cents and quarter cents, no silver or copper coins, except those mentioned below, shall be coined at the mints in British India:—

Silver Coins.

A rupee to be called the Government rupee.
A half rupee.
A quarter rupee or four-anna piece.
An eighth of a rupee or two-anna piece.

Copper Coins.

A double pice or half anna.
A pice or quarter anna.
A pie, being one-third of a pice, or one-twelfth of an anna.

III. The rupee so coined shall be of the same weight and standard as those provided for the Company's rupee by the said Act XVII of 1835, that is to say, the weight shall be 180 grains troy, and the standard as follows:—

$\frac{11}{12}$th or 165 grains of pure silver.
$\frac{1}{12}$th or 15 grains of alloy.

The other silver coins shall be of proportionate weight and of the same standard.

IV. The copper coins so coined shall be of the weight prescribed for coins of the same denominations respectively by Acts XXI of 1835 and XI of 1854, that is to say :—

The double pice shall weigh	200 grs. troy.
The pice	100 ,,
The half pice	50 ,,
The pie	$33\frac{1}{3}$,,

V. Until the Governor-General in Council shall otherwise order under the power hereinafter reserved, the silver and copper coins so coined shall bear on the obverse the likeness and the name of Queen Victoria and the inscription VICTORIA QUEEN, and on the reverse the designation of the coins in English, filled by the word INDIA, with such date and embellishments on each coins as the Governor-General in Council shall from time to time direct.

II.—CATALOGUE OF COINS IN THE MADRAS MUSEUM.

ENGLISH EAST INDIA COMPANY.

No.	Date.	Obverse.	Reverse.
		A. COINS WITH DATE.	
		MADRAS COPPER.	
1	1722	Orb and cross inscribed C.C.E., surrounded by a radiate border. [Pl. i, 1.]	Date 1722, with wavy line above and below, surrounded by a beaded circle.
2	1733	Bale-mark of the Company.	Date 1733. [Pl. i, 2.]
3	1733	„	„ [Pl. i, 3.]
4	1736	„	Date 1736. [Pl. i, 4.]
5	1737	„	Date 1737, surrounded by a beaded circle. [Pl. i, 5.]
6	1755	Orb and cross inscribed C.C.E., surrounded by a radiate border.	Date 1755, with wavy line above and below. [Pl. i, 6.]
7	1755	„	„ but traces of a beaded circle.
8	1755	„	„
9	1756	„	„ but date *x*756. [Pl. i, 7.]
10	176*x*	„	„ but date 176*x*.
11	176*x*	„	„
12	177*x*	„	„ but date 177*x*.
13	177*x*	„	„
		BOMBAY COPPER DOUBLE PICE.	
14-15	1777	A crown with BOMB 1777 below it.	Bale-mark of the Company. [Pl. xv, 1.]

No.	Date.	Obverse.	Reverse.
		A. COINS WITH DATE—*continued.*	
		BOMBAY COPPER DOUBLE PICE—*continued.*	
16–25	177*x*	„ but date indistinct.	„ [Pl. xv, 2.]
		BOMBAY COPPER PICE.	
26	1777	Inscription 1 PICE BOMBAY 1777.	Bale-mark of the Company. [Pl. xv, 3.]
27–35	177*x*	„ but date indistinct.	„ [Pl. xi, 13.]
		MADRAS COPPER.	
36	1786	Orb and cross inscribed C.C. E., surrounded by a radiate border.	Date 1786, with wavy line above and below. [Pl. i, 8.]
		BOMBAY 20 CASH.	
		(*a*). GILT PROOF.	
37	1791	Bale-mark of the Company with date 1791 below.	A balance with the word عدل between the scales.
		(OBLIQUE MILLING.)	
		(*b*). BRONZE PROOF.	
38	1791	„	„
		BOMBAY 15 CASH.	
		BRONZE PROOF.	
39	1791	„	„
40	1791	„	„
		BOMBAY 10 CASH.	
		COPPER.	
41	1791	„	„ [Pl. i, 9.]

No.	Date.	Obverse.	Reverse.
		A. COINS WITH DATE—*continued.*	
		BOMBAY 5 CASH.	
		(*a*). Gilt Proof.	
42	1791	Bale-mark of the Company with date 1791 below.	A balance with the word عدل between the scales.
		(*b*). Bronze Proof.	
43	1791	„	„
		BOMBAY 20 CASH.	
		(*a*). Copper.	
44	1794	„	„ [Pl. i, 10.]
		(*b*). Gilt Proof.	
45	1794	„	„
		BOMBAY 10 CASH.	
		(*a*). Copper.	
46	1794	„	„
		(*b*). Gilt Proof.	
47	1794	„	„
		BOMBAY 5 CASH.	
		Gilt Proof.	
48	1794	„	„

No.	Date.	Obverse.	Reverse.
		A. COINS WITH DATE—*continued.*	
		MADRAS $\frac{1}{48}$ RUPEE.[1]	
		(*a*). COPPER.	
49	1794	The arms of the Company with 48 TO ONE RUPEE below. The motto AUSPICIO REGIS ET SENATUS ANGLIÆ incuse upon a broad rim.	Bale-mark of the Company. The legend UNITED EAST INDIA COMPANY 1794 incuse upon a broad rim.
		The edge inscribed with the legend ENGLISH UNITED EAST INDIA COMPANY.	
		(*b*). GILT PROOF.	
50	1794	"	"
		(*c*). BRONZE PROOF.	
51	1794	"	"
		MADRAS $\frac{1}{96}$ RUPEE.	
		BRONZE PROOF.	
52	1794	" but 96 TO ONE RUPEE.	"
		MADRAS $\frac{1}{48}$ RUPEE.	
		COPPER.	
53	1797	Same as No. 49.	Same as No 49 except date.
		MADRAS $\frac{1}{96}$ RUPEE.	
		(*a*). COPPER.	
54	1797	Same as No. 52.	Same as No. 52 except date.

[1] This and the following coins of the same type are attributed by weight to the 'Cirkars in der Präsidentschaft Madras,' and Atkins writes concerning them: "In the following series an attempt has evidently been made to assimilate the Mohammedan with the Hindu monetary systems, as the 48th part of a Rupee is just equal to the Faluce or piece of 20 Cash. They were struck for the Circars, a large district on the coast of the Bay of Bengal to the north of the Carnatic country, and thus in a measure connecting Madras with Bengal."

A. COINS WITH DATE—*continued.*

(*b*). Gilt Proof.

No.	Date.	Obverse.	Reverse.
55	1797	Same as No. 52.	Same as No. 52 except date.

MADRAS COPPER CASH.

No.	Date.	Obverse.	Reverse.
56	۱۲۱۲	Bale-mark of the Company surrounded by a beaded circle.	Date ۱۲۱۲. [Pl. i, 11.]

TELLICHERRY SILVER.

No.	Date.	Obverse.	Reverse.
57	1799 ?	T. 99, and Persian inscription, surrounded by a beaded circle.	Persian inscription surrounded by a beaded circle. [Pl. ii, 1.]
58	1799 ?	,,	,, [Pl. ii, 2.]

MADRAS COPPER.

No.	Date.	Obverse.	Reverse.
59	1801	Orb and cross inscribed C.C. E. surrounded by a radiate border.	Date x801 with wavy line above and below. [Pl. i, 12.]
60	1801	,,	,,
61	180x	,, [Pl. i, 13.]	,,

MADRAS COPPER 2 DUBS.

No.	Date.	Obverse.	Reverse.
62	1801	۱۸۰۱ عیسوی دو فلوس هانربل کمپنی ("Christian year 1801. Two *falūs* of the Honorable Company") surrounded by a serrated circle.	Inscription in Telugu "Two Dubs of the Company:" 2 DUBS: surrounded by a serrated circle. [Pl. ii, 3.]

MADRAS COPPER ½ DUB.

No.	Date.	Obverse.	Reverse.
63	1801	۱۸۰۱ عیسوی فلوس هانربل کمپنی ("Christian year 1801. *Falūs* of the Honorable Company.")	Inscription in Telugu "Half Dub of the Company:" ½ DUB. [Pl. ii, 4, 5.]
64	1801	,,	,,

No.	Date.	Obverse.	Reverse.
		A. COINS WITH DATE—*continued.*	
		BOMBAY COPPER DOUBLE PICE.	
65	1802	Bale-mark of the Company with date 1802 below, surrounded by a serrated circle.	A balance with the word عدل between the scales, surrounded by a serrated circle.
66	1803	„ but date 1803.	„
		MADRAS COPPER 1 CASH.	
67	1803	Bale-mark of the Company.	Date 1803. [Pl. ii, 6.]
68	1803	„	„ [Pl. ii, 7.]
		MADRAS 1 CASH.[1]	
		(*a*). COPPER.	
69	1803	Lion l, carrying a crown, with date 1803 below. Plain rim on face.	كاس ("*kās*") 1 CASH. Plain rim on face. [Pl. ii, 8.]
70	1803	„	„
		(*b*). SILVER PROOF.	
71	1803	„	„
72	1803	„	„

[1] "These pieces occur as proofs in silver, bronzed, and gilt. They were made in England by Messrs. Boulton and Vatt, and it is said that No. 137 (= Nos. 69, 70) is the smallest coin ever struck in collar." Atkins.

A. COINS WITH DATE—*continued*.

MADRAS COPPER 10 CASH.

No.	Date.	Obverse.	Reverse.
73	1803	The arms of the Company with EAST INDIA COMPANY above, and date 1803 below: serrated rim on face.	ده کاس دو فلوس است ("Ten *kās* make two *falūs*") X CASH: serrated rim on face. [Pl. ii, 9.]
74	1803	,,	,,

MADRAS COPPER 5 CASH.

No.	Date.	Obverse.	Reverse.
75	1803	,,	پنج کاس یکفلوس است ("Five *kās* make one *falūs*") V CASH: serrated rim on face. [Pl. ii, 10.]
76	1803	,,	,,

BOMBAY 20 CASH.

Gilt Proof.

No.	Date.	Obverse.	Reverse.
77	1804	,, but date 1804.	A balance with the word عدل between the scales, and date ١٢١٩ beneath surrounded by a beaded circle.

BOMBAY 10 CASH.

(*a*). Copper.

No.	Date.	Obverse.	Reverse.
78	1804	,,	,, [Pl. ii. 11.]

(*b*). Gilt Proof.

No.	Date.	Obverse.	Reverse.
79	1804	,,	,,

No.	Date.	Obverse.	Reverse.
		A. COINS WITH DATE—*continued.*	
		BOMBAY 5 CASH.	
		(*a*). COPPER.	
80	1804	The arms of the Company with EAST INDIA COMPANY above, but date 1804. [Pl. iii, 1.]	A balance with the word عدل between the scales, and date ١٢١٩ beneath; surrounded by a beaded circle.
81	1804	"	"
		(*b*). GILT PROOF.	
82	1804	"	"
		SILVER, TELLICHERRY.	
83	1805	A balance with the letter T between the scales, and date 1805 below.	Persian inscription. [Pl. iii, 2.]
84	1805	"	"
85	1805	" [Pl. iii, 3.]	"
		GOLD, TELLICHERRY.	
86	180*x*	T. 99, Persian inscription, and date 180*x*: surrounded by a beaded circle. [Pl. iii, 4.]	Persian inscription, surrounded by a beaded circle.
		MADRAS COPPER.	
87	1807	Bale-mark of the Company.	Date 1807. [Pl. iii, 5.]
88	1807	"	"

A. COINS WITH DATE—*continued.*

MADRAS COPPER 3 DUBS.

No.	Date.	Obverse.	Reverse.
89	1807	۱۸۰۷ عیسوی این سکه سه فلوس هانربل کمپنی یك فلم خورد است ("Christian year 1807. This coin, three *falūs* of the Honorable Company, makes one little fanam.")	In centre within circle, inscription in Telugu "Three new dubs and one little fanam." The same inscription in Tamil round margin. [Pl. iii, 7.]

MADRAS COPPER ½ DUB.

No.	Date.	Obverse.	Reverse.
90	1807	۱۸۰۷ عیسوی نیم فلوس هانربل کمپنی ("Christian year 1807. Half *falūs* of the Honorable Company.")	In centre within circle inscription in Telugu "Company's half dub." The same inscription in Tamil round margin. [Pl. xv, 4.]
91	1807	”	”

MADRAS COPPER 20 CASH.

No.	Date.	Obverse.	Reverse.
92	1808	The arms of the Company with EAST INDIA COMPANY above, and date 1808 below: serrated rim on face.	بیست کاس چهار فلوس است ("Twenty *kās* make four *falūs*") XX CASH: serrated rim on face. [Pl. iii, 6.]
93	1808	”	”

MADRAS COPPER 10 CASH.

No.	Date.	Obverse.	Reverse.
94	1808	”	ده کاس دو فلوس است ("Ten *kās* make two *falūs*") X CASH: serrated rim on face.
95	1808	”	”

No.	Date.	Obverse.	Reverse.
		A. COINS WITH DATE—*continued.*	
		BENGAL 1 PIE.	
		COPPER PROOF.	
96	1809	The arms of the Company, with ONE PIE above, and date 1809 below: surrounded by a beaded circle.	The value of the coin "One Pai Sikka" in Persian, Nagárí, and Bengáli: surrounded by a beaded circle. [Pl. xv, 5.]
		BENGAL ½ PIE.	
		COPPER PROOF.	
97	1809	,,	,, but value of coin "Half Pai Sikka." [Pl. xv, 6.]
		BOMBAY COPPER PICE.	
98	1809	Bale-mark of the Company with date 1809 below.	A balance with the word عدل between the scales.
99	1810	,, but date 1810.	,,
100	1813	,, but date 1813.	,,
101	1815	,, but date 1815.	,,
102	1815	,, ,,	,,
		BOMBAY COPPER 4 PICE.	
103	1816	,, but date 1816.	A balance with the word عدل and numeral 4 between the scales. [Pl. iii, 8.]
		BOMBAY COPPER DOUBLE PICE.	
104	1816	,, ,, [Pl. iii, 9.]	,, but no numeral.
		BOMBAY COPPER PICE.	
105	1816	,, ,,	,, [Pl. iii, 10.]

No.	Date.	Obverse.	Reverse.
		A. COINS WITH DATE—*continued.*	
		BOMBAY COPPER DOUBLE PICE.	
106	1819	Bale-mark of the Company, but date 1819.	A balance with the word عدل but no numeral.
		BOMBAY COPPER PICE.	
107	1820	„ but date 1820.	„
		BOMBAY COPPER PICE.	
108	1821	Bale-mark of the Company.	A balance with inscription in Nágarí पैसा (“*Paisá*”) between the scales, and date १८२१ below. [Pl. xv, 7.]
		BOMBAY COPPER ½ PICE.	
109	1821	„ and traces of date 18 *xx*.	A balance with inscription in Nágarí अधपैसा (“*Half Paisá*”) between the scales, and date १८२१ below. [Pl. iv, 1.]
		BOMBAY COPPER PICE.	
110	18*xx*	Bale-mark of the Company, date illegible.	A balance with the word عدل between the scales. [Pl. iv, 4.]
111	1825	Bale-mark of the Company with date 1825 below.	„ [Pl. iv, 2.]
112	1825	„	„
		BOMBAY COPPER ½ PICE.	
113	1825	„	„ [Pl. iv, 3.]
		BOMBAY COPPER ¼ PICE.	
114	1825	„	„

No.	Date.	Obverse.	Reverse.
		A. COINS WITH DATE—*continued.*	
		BENGAL COPPER 4 PAÍ.	
115	1825	The arms of the Company and date 1825: serrated rim on face.	Inscription 4 چهار پائی[1] سنہ ١٢٤٠ within a wreath: serrated rim on face. [Pl. iv, 5.]
		BENGAL COPPER 2 PAÍ.	
116	1825	,,	,, but inscription 2 دو پائی سنہ ١٢٤٠.[2] [Pl. iv, 6.]
117	1825	,,	,,
		BENGAL COPPER 1 PAÍ.	
118	1825	,,	,, but inscription 1 یک پائی سنہ ١٢٤٠.[3] [Pl. iv, 7.
119	1825	,,	,,
		BOMBAY COPPER ¼ ANNA.	
120	1833	The arms of the Company and date 1833: plain rim on face.	A balance with the word عدل between the scales QUARTER ANNA above and date ١٢٣٩ below plain rim on face. [Pl. iv, 8.
121	1833	,,	,,
		BOMBAY COPPER 1 PIE.	
122	1833	The arms of the Company and date 1833: plain rim on face.	A balance with the wor عدل between the scales PIE above, and date ١٢٤٠ below: plain rim o face. [Pl. iv, 9.
123	1833	,,	,,
		BOMBAY COPPER ½ ANNA.	
124	1834	The arms of the Company with EAST INDIA COMPANY above, and date 1834 below: plain rim on face.	A balance with the wor عدل between the scale HALF ANNA above, an date ١٢٣٩ below: plai rim on face. [Pl. iv, 10.

[1] "Four *paí*, year 1240."
[2] "Two *paí*, year 1240."
[3] "One *paí*, year 1240."

No.	Date.	Obverse.	Reverse.
		A. COINS WITH DATE—*continued.*	
		GOLD.	
		DOUBLE MOHUR.	
125	1835	Bust of the King r: WILLIAM IV KING above, and date 1835 below: dotted rim on face.	Lion and Palm Tree: EAST INDIA COMPANY above, TWO MOHURS دو اشرفی[1] below: dotted rim on face.
		(STRAIGHT MILLING.)	
			[Pl. v, 1.]
		SINGLE MOHUR.	
126	1835	,,	,, but ONE MOHUR یک اشرفی[2]
			[Pl. v, 2.]
		SILVER.	
		1 RUPEE.	
127	1835	Bust of the King r: WILLIAM IV KING: dotted rim on face.	Inscription ONE RUPEE یک روپیه[3] within a wreath EAST INDIA COMPANY 1835, around: dotted rim on face.
		(STRAIGHT MILLING.)	
			[Pl. v, 3.]
128	1835	,,	,,
		½ RUPEE.	
129	1835	,,	,, but inscription within the wreath HALF RUPEE هشت آنه[4]
		(STRAIGHT MILLING.)	
			[Pl. v, 4.]
130	1835	,,	,,

[1] "Two ashrafí."
[2] "One ashrafí."
[3] "One rupee."
[4] "Eight annas."

No.	Date.	Obverse.	Reverse.
		A. COINS WITH DATE—*continued.*	
		SILVER—*continued.*	
		¼ RUPEE.	
131	1835	Bust of the King r: WILLIAM IV KING: dotted rim on face.	Dotted rim on face, but inscription within the wreath ¼ RUPEE چهار آنه [1]
		(STRAIGHT MILLING.)	
132	1835	,,	,, [Pl. v, 5.]
		COPPER.	
		½ ANNA.	
133	1835	The arms of the Company and date 1835: plain rim on face.	Inscription دو پائی [2] HALF ANNA within a wreath: EAST INDIA COMPANY around: plain rim on face. [Pl. v, 6.]
134	1835	,,	,,
		¼ ANNA.	
135	1835	,,	,, but inscription within the wreath پائی ایک [3] ONE QUARTER ANNA. [Pl. v, 7.]
136	1835	,,	,,
		$\frac{1}{12}$ ANNA.	
137	1835	,,	,, but inscription within the wreath $\frac{1}{12}$ ANNA ثلث پائی [4] [Pl. v, 8.]
138	1835	,,	,,

[1] "Four annas."
[2] "Two *pai*."
[3] "One *pai*."
[4] "One-third *pai*."

No.	Date.	Obverse.	Reverse.
		A. COINS WITH DATE—*continued.*	
		SILVER—*continued.*	
		1 RUPEE.	
139	1840	Bust of the Queen l: VICTORIA QUEEN: serrated rim on face.	Inscription ONE RUPEE یك روپیه within a wreath: EAST INDIA COMPANY 1840 around: serrated rim on face.
		(STRAIGHT MILLING.)	
140	1840	,,	,,
		½ RUPEE.	
141	1840	,,	,, but inscription within the wreath HALF RUPEE هشت آنه
		(STRAIGHT MILLING.)	
142	1840	,,	,,
		¼ RUPEE.	
143	1840	,,	,, but inscription within the wreath ¼ RUPEE چهار آنه
		(STRAIGHT MILLING.)	
144	1840	,,	,,
		GOLD.	
		SINGLE MOHUR.	
145	1841	Bust of Queen Victoria l: VICTORIA QUEEN: serrated rim on face.	Lion and Palm Tree: EAST INDIA COMPANY above, ONE MOHUR یك اشرفی below: serrated rim on face.

No.	Date.	Obverse.	Reverse.
		A. COINS WITH DATE—*continued.*	
		SILVER—*continued.*	
		2 ANNAS.	
146	1841	Bust of Queen Victoria l: VICTORIA QUEEN: serrated rim on face.	Serrated rim on face, but inscription within the wreath TWO ANNAS دو آنه[1] and date 1841.
		(No Milling.)	
147	1841	"	" [Pl. v, 9.]
		COPPER.	
		1 CENT.	
148	1845	Bust of the Queen l: and inscription VICTORIA QUEEN: plain rim on face.	Inscription ONE CENT within a wreath: EAST INDIA COMPANY, 1845, around: serrated rim on face.
149	1845	"	"
		½ CENT.	
150	1845	"	" but inscription within the wreath HALF CENT.
151	1845	"	"
		¼ CENT.	
152	1845	"	" but inscription within the wreath QUARTER CENT.
		SILVER.	
		1 RUPEE.	
153	1849	Bust of the Queen l: VICTORIA QUEEN: serrated rim on face.	Inscription ONE RUPEE ایک روپیہ within a wreath: EAST INDIA COMPANY, 1849, around: serrated rim on face.

[1] "Two annas."

No.	Date.	Obverse.	Reverse.
		A. COINS WITH DATE—*continued.*	
		½ RUPEE.	
154	1849	Bust of the Queen l: VICTORIA QUEEN: serrated rim on face.	Serrated rim on face, but inscription within the wreath HALF RUPEE هشت آنه.
		(STRAIGHT MILLING.)	
		¼ RUPEE.	
155	1849	,,	,, but inscription within the wreath ¼ RUPEE چهار آنه.
		(STRAIGHT MILLING.)	
		2 ANNAS.	
156	1849	,,	,, but inscription within the wreath TWO ANNAS.
		(NO MILLING.)	
		COPPER.	
		¼ ANNA.	
157	1853	The arms of the Company and date 1853: serrated rim on face.	Inscription یک پائی ONE QUARTER ANNA within a wreath: EAST INDIA COMPANY around: serrated rim on face.
		½ PICE.	
158	1853	,, but plain rim on face.	,, but inscription ½ PICE within the wreath and plain rim on face.
159	1853	,,	,,

No.	Mint: Date.	Obverse.	Reverse.
		B. COINS STRUCK IN THE NAME OF NATIVE PRINCES.	
		MURSHIDÁBÁD.	
		GOLD MOHUR.	
		(OBLIQUE MILLING.)	
1	Murshidábád ۱۲۰۲	حامی دین محمد سایۂ فضل الہ سکہ زد بر هفت کشور شاه عالم بادشاه ۱۲۰۲ ("Defender of the Muhammadan faith, Reflection of Divine Excellence, the Emperor Sháh Alam has struck this coin to be current throughout the seven climes. 1202") (Prinsep.)	ضرب مرشد آباد سنہ ۱۹ جلوس میمنت مانوس ("Struck at Murshidábád in the 19th year of his fortunate reign.") [Pl. vi, 1.]
1. 1	Murshidábád ۱۲۰۲	"	"
		GOLD MOHUR.	
		(STRAIGHT MILLING.)	
1. 2	Murshidábád ۱۲۰۲	"	"
		GOLD ONE-QUARTER MOHUR.	
		(OBLIQUE MILLING.)	
2	Murshidábád ۱۲۰۳	۱۲۰۳ سکہ شاه عالم بادشاه ("1204. Coin of the Emperor Sháh Álam.")	ضرب مرشد آباد سنہ ۱۹ ("Struck at Murshidábád in the 19th year.") [Pl. vi, 2.]
3	Murshidábád ۱۲۰۳	"	"
		RUPEE.	
		(OBLIQUE MILLING.)	
4	Murshidábád *Sun* 19.	حامی دین محمد سایۂ فضل الہ سکہ زد بر هفت کشور شاه عالم بادشاه ("Defender of the Muhammadan faith, Reflection of Divine Excellence, the Emperor Sháh Alam has struck this coin to be current throughout the seven climes.")	ضرب مرشد آباد سنہ ۱۹ جلوس میمنت مانوس ("Struck at Murshidábád in the 19th year of his fortunate reign.")

No.	Mint: Date.	Obverse.	Reverse.
		B. COINS STRUCK IN THE NAME OF NATIVE PRINCES—*continued.*	
		RUPEE—*continued.*	
		(Straight Milling.)	
5	Murshidábád *Sun* 19.	Same legend as 4: dotted rim on the face.	Same legend as 4: dotted rim on the face. [Pl. vi, 3.]
6	Murshidábád *Sun* 19.	Same legend: but plain rim on face.	Same legend: but plain rim on face.
		HALF RUPEE.	
		(Straight Milling.)	
7	Murshidábád *Sun* 19.	Same legend: but serrated rim on face.	Same legend: but serrated rim on face. [Pl. vi, 4.]
		QUARTER RUPEE.	
		(Straight Milling.)	
8	Murshidábád ۱۲۰۴	۱۲۰۴ سکه شاه‌عالم بادشاه ("1204. Coin of the Emperor Sháh Alam:") serrated rim on face.	ضرب مرشد آباد سنه ۱۹ (" Struck at Murshidábád in the 19th year:") serrated rim on face. [Pl. vi, 5.]
		RUPEE.	
		(Without Milling.)	
9	Murshidábád *Sun* 19.	حامی دین محمد سایهٔ فضل اله سکه زد بر هفت کشور شاه‌عالم بادشاه ("Defender of the Muhammadan faith, Reflection of Divine Excellence, the Emperor Sháh Álam has struck this coin to be current throughout the seven climes.")	ضرب مرشد آباد سنه ۱۹ جلوس میمنت مانوس ("Struck at Murshidábád in the 19th year of his fortunate reign.") [Pl. vi, 6.]
10	Murshidábád *Sun* 19.	Same legend as 9: serrated rim on the face.	Same legend as 9: serrated rim on the face.

B. COINS STRUCK IN THE NAME OF NATIVE PRINCES—*continued.*

HALF RUPEE.

(WITHOUT MILLING.)

No.	Mint : Date.	Obverse.	Reverse.
11	Murshidábád *Sun* 19.	Same as 9.	Same as 9. [Pl. vi, 7.]

QUARTER RUPEE.

(WITHOUT MILLING.)

No.	Mint : Date.	Obverse.	Reverse.
12	Murshidábád ۱۲۰۴	۱۲۰۴ سکه شاه عالم بادشاه ("1204. Coin of the Emperor Sháh Álam.")	ضرب مرشد آباد سنه ۱۹ ("Struck at Murshidábád in the 19th year.") [Pl. vi, 8.]

FARUKHÁBÁD.

RUPEE.[1]

(OBLIQUE MILLING.)

No.	Mint : Date.	Obverse.	Reverse.
13	Farukhábád *Sun* 45.	حامی دین محمد سایهٔ فضل اله سکه زد بر هفت کشور شاه عالم بادشاه ("Defender of the Muhammadan faith, Reflection of Divine Excellence, the Emperor Sháh Álam has struck this coin to be current throughout the seven climes.")	ضرب فرخ آباد سنه ۴۵ جلوس میمنت مانوس ("Struck at Farukhábád in the 45th year of his prosperous reign.") [Pl. vii, 1.]

RUPEE.

(STRAIGHT MILLING.)

No.	Mint : Date.	Obverse.	Reverse.
14	Farukhábád *Sun* 45.	"	" [Pl. vii, 2.]
15	Farukhábád *Sun* 45.	"	"

[1] 45th sun Lucknow rupee of Reg. XLV, 1803.

No.	Mint : Date.	Obverse.	Reverse.
		B. COINS STRUCK IN THE NAME OF NATIVE PRINCES—*continued.*	
		RUPEE—*continued.*	
		(WITHOUT MILLING.)	
16	Farukhábád *Sun* 45.	Same legend as 13: plain rim on face.	Same legend as 13: plain rim on face.
			[Pl. vii, 3.]
17	Farukhábád *Sun* 45.	,,	,,
		HALF RUPEE.	
		(WITHOUT MILLING.)	
18	Farukhábád *Sun* 45.	,,	,,
			[Pl. vii, 4.]
19	Farukhábád *Sun* 45.	,,	,,
			[Pl. vii, 5.]
		QUARTER RUPEE.	
		(WITHOUT MILLING.)	
20	Farukhábád ۱۲۰۴	۱۲۰۴ سکه شاه عالم بادشاه ("1204. Coin of the Emperor Sháh Álam:") plain rim on face.	ضرب فرخ آباد سنه ۴۵ ("Struck at Farukhábád in the 45th year:") plain rim on face.
			[Pl. vii, 6.]
21	Farukhábád ۱۲۰۴	,,	,,
		BENARES.	
		RUPEE.	
		(OBLIQUE MILLING.)	
22	Benares ۱۲۲۹	حامی دین محمد سایهٔ فضل اله سکه زد بر هفت کشور شاه عالم بادشاه سنه ۱۲۲۹ ("Defender of the Muhammadan faith, Reflection of Divine Excellence, the Emperor Sháh Alam has struck this coin to be current throughout the seven climes. 1229.")	ضرب محمد آباد بنارس جلوس میمنت مانوس سنه ۱۷/۳۹ ("Struck at *Muhammadábád*, Benares, in the year ۱۷/۳۹ of his fortunate reign.")
			[Pl. vii, 7.]

No.	Mint : Date.	Obverse.	Reverse.
		B. COINS STRUCK IN THE NAME OF NATIVE PRINCES—*continued.*	
		HALF RUPEE.	
		(OBLIQUE MILLING.)	
23	Benares ١٢٢٩	"	" [Pl. vii, 1.]
		QUARTER RUPEE.	
		(OBLIQUE MILLING.)	
24	Benares ١٢٢٩	١٢٢٩ سكه شاه عالم بادشاه ("1229. Coin of the Emperor Sháh Alam.")	ضرب بنارس سنه ١٧٣٩ ("Struck at Benares in the year 1749.") [Pl. vii, 8.]
		TRISOOLEE PICE.	
25	Benares *Sun* ٣٧	Value of the coin "*One pai*" in Persian and Bengálí: Mint mark a *trisula.*	شاه عالم بادشاه جلوس سنه ٣٧ Mint mark a *trisula.* [Pl. xvi 1.]
26	Benares *Sun* ٣٧	"	"
27	Benares *Sun* ٣٧	"	"
28	Benares *Sun* ٣٧	"	"
29	Benares *Sun* ٣٥	"	شاه عالم بادشاه جلوس سنه ٣٥ Mint mark a *trisula.* [Pl. xvi, 2.]

No.	Mint : Date.	Obverse.	Reverse.
		B. COINS STRUCK IN THE NAME OF NATIVE PRINCES—*continued.*	
		SURAT.	
		RUPEE.	
		(Straight Milling.)	
30	Surat ۱۲۱۵	سکه مبارک شاه عالم بادشاه غازی سنه ۱۲۱۵ ("The auspicious coin of the great Emperor Shah Álam, 1215:") surrounded by lined circle.	ضرب سورت سنه ۴۶ جلوس میمنت مانوس ("Struck at Surat in the 46th year of his propitious reign:") surrounded by lined circle. [Pl. viii, 2.]
31	Surat ۱۲۱۵	"	"
		RUPEE.	
		(Without Milling.)	
32	Surat ۱۲۱۵	Same legend as 25: but serrated rim on face.	Same legend as 25: but serrated rim on face. [Pl. viii, 3.]
33	Surat ۱۲۱۵	"	"
		HALF RUPEE.	
		(Without Milling.)	
34	Surat ۱۲۱۵	"	" [Pl. viii, 4.
35	Surat ۱۲۱۵	"	"
		QUARTER RUPEE.	
		(Without Milling.)	
36	Surat ۱۲۱۵	Same legend as 27: but plain rim on face.	Same legend as 27: but plain rim on face. [Pl. viii, 5.]
37	Surat ۱۲۱۵	"	"

No.	Mint : Date.	Obverse.	Reverse.
		B. COINS STRUCK IN THE NAME OF NATIVE PRINCES—*continued.*	
		THICK GOLD MOHUR.	
38	Surat	. . . . . بادشاه . . . . A small crown.	. . . . ۳ جلوس . . . . . [Pl. xvi, 3.]
		THIN RUPEE.[1]	
39	Surat	. . . . . بادشاه غا	. . . . جلوس . . . . . [Pl. xvi, 4.]
		THICK RUPEE.	
40	Surat, 1825	. . . . . . ۳ بادشاه . . . . A small crown.	. . . . . جلوس . . . . . Date 1825 incuse. [Pl. xvi, 5.]
41	"	"	"
		THICK HALF RUPEE.	
42	"	"	" [Pl. xvi, 6.]
		ARCOT.[2]	
		DOUBLE RUPEE.	
		(OBLIQUE MILLING.)	
43	Arcot ۱۱۷۲	۱۱۷۲ سکه مبارک بادشاه غازی عزیزالدین محمد عالمگیر ("The auspicious coin of the noble Monarch Áziz-ud-dín Muhammad Álamgír, 1172:") serrated rim on face.	ضرب ارکاٹ سنه ۶ جلوس میمنت مانوس ("Struck at Arkát in the 6th year of his propitious reign:") serrated rim on face. [Pl. ix, 1.]
44	Arcot ۱۱۷۲	"	"

[1] "The improved '*Surat*' Rupee, showing more of legend and better struck, coined both at Calcutta and Bombay, 1800 to 1818. Those struck at Bombay bear as mint mark a small crown." Atkins.

[2] Arcot rupees and their divisions were struck not only at the Madras Mint, but also at the Calcutta Mint, the latter being known as Calcutta-Arcot rupees, and distinguished from the former by bearing a rose as a mint mark instead of a lotus flower. Both types are represented in the following series. (*Vide* pl. ix, x.)

No.	Mint: Date.	Obverse.	Reverse.
		B. COINS STRUCK IN THE NAME OF NATIVE PRINCES—*continued.*	
		RUPEE.	
		(Oblique Milling.)	
45	Arcot ۱۱۷۲	Same legend as 33: surrounded by a lined circle.	Same legend as 33: surrounded by a lined circle. [Pl. ix, 2.]
46	Arcot ۱۱۷۲	"	"
		DOUBLE ANNA.	
		(Oblique Milling.)	
47	Arcot ۱۱۷۲	۱۱۷۲ سکہ عالمگیر بادشاہ ("1172. Coin of the Emperor Alamgír:") surrounded by a lined circle.	ضرب ارکاٹ سنہ ۶ ("Struck at *Arkát* in the 6th year:") surrounded by a lined circle. [Pl. ix, 3.]
48	Arcot ۱۱۷۲	"	"
		SINGLE ANNA.	
		(Oblique Milling.)	
49	Arcot ۱۱۷۲	"	" [Pl. ix, 4.]
50	Arcot ۱۱۷۲	"	"

No.	Mint : Date.	Obverse.	Reverse.
		B. COINS STRUCK IN THE NAME OF NATIVE PRINCES—*continued.*	
		RUPEE.	
		(STRAIGHT MILLING.)	
51	Arcot ۱۱۷۲	۱۱۷۲ سکه مبارک بادشاه غازی عزیزالدین محمد عالمگیر ("The auspicious coin of the noble Monarch, Ázíz-ud-dín Muhammad Álamgír 1172:") dotted rim on face.	ضرب ارکاٹ سنه ۶ جلوس میمنت مانوس ("Struck at *Arkót* in the 6th year of his propitious reign:") dotted rim on face. [Pl. ix, 5.]
52	Arcot ۱۱۷۲	"	"
		HALF RUPEE.	
		(STRAIGHT MILLING.)	
53	Arcot ۱۱۷۲	"	" [Pl. ix, 6.]
54	Arcot ۱۱۷۲	"	"
		QUARTER RUPEE.	
		(STRAIGHT MILLING.)	
55	Arcot ۱۱۷۲	"	" [Pl. ix, 7.]
56	Arcot ۱۱۷۲	"	"
		GOLD MOHUR.	
		(INDENTED CORD MILLING.)	
57	Arcot ۱۱۷۲	۱۱۷۲ سکه مبارک بادشاه غازی عزیزالدین محمد عالمگیر ("The auspicious coin of the noble Monarch Azíz-ud-dín Muhammad Álamgír, 1172:") dotted rim on face.	ضرب ارکاٹ سنه ۶ جلوس میمنت مانوس ("Struck at Arkát in the 6th year of his propitious reign:") dotted rim on face. [Pl. x, 1.]

No.	Mint: Date.	Obverse.	Reverse.
		B. COINS STRUCK IN THE NAME OF NATIVE PRINCES—*continued.*	
		GOLD MOHUR—*continued.*	
		(Indented Cord Milling.)	
58	Arcot ۱۱۷۲	”	”
		HALF MOHUR.	
		(Indented Cord Milling.)	
59	Arcot ۱۱۷۲	”	” [Pl. x, 2.]
		RUPEE.	
		(Indented Cord Milling.)	
60	Arcot ۱۱۷۲	”	” [Pl. x, 3.]
61	Arcot ۱۱۷۲	”	”
		HALF RUPEE.	
		(Indented Cord Milling.)	
62	Arcot ۱۱۷۲	”	” [Pl. x, 4].
		QUARTER RUPEE.	
		(Indented Cord Milling.)	
63	Arcot ۱۱۷۲	۱۱۷۲ سکہ عالمگیر بادشاہ ("1172. Coin of the Emperor Alamgír:") dotted rim on face.	ضرب ارکات سنہ ۶ ("Struck at Arkát in the 6th year:") dotted rim on face. [Pl. x, 5.]

No.	Mint: Date.	Obverse.	Reverse.
		B. COINS STRUCK IN THE NAME OF NATIVE PRINCES—*continued.*	
		GOLD MOHUR.	
		(No Milling.)	
64	Arcot ۱۲۱۴	سکه زد بر هفت کشور سایهٔ فضل اله حامی دین محمد شاه عالم بادشاه ("Defender of the Muhammadan faith, Reflection of Divine Excellence, the Emperor Sháh Alam struck this coin to be current throughout the seven climates.[1] 1214.")	ضرب ارکاٹ سنه ۵۹ جلوس میمنت مانوس ("Struck at Arkát in the 59th (?) year of the auspicious reign."). [Pl. x, 6.]
		THICK RUPEE.	
		(Without Milling.)	
65	Arcot ۱۲۱۴	"	" but year 44. [Pl. x, 7.]
		THICK RUPEE.	
		(Without Milling.)	
66	Arcot	Traces of . . . . بادشاه	Lotus, and traces of سنه جلوس ارکاٹ [Pl. x, 8.]
67	Arcot	"	"

[1] "When Timur, establishing his throne in India, overcame the Kings of Cashmeer, Bengal, Decan, Gudjraat, Lahore, Poorub, and Paishoor, he united the kingdoms, and called himself conqueror and sovereign of the seven climates or countries." Moor, Narrative of Little's Detachment, App. p. 472.

No.	Obverse.	Reverse.
	C. COINS WITHOUT DATE.	
	GOLD.	
	MADRAS THREE-SWAMI PAGODA.[1]	
1	Standing figures of Venkatesvara and his two wives.	Granulated surface. [Pl. xi, 1.]
2	”	”
3	”	”
	MADRAS PORTO NOVO OR SCOTT PAGODA.	
4	Figure of Vishnu.	Granulated surface. [Pl. xi, 2.]
	COPPER.[2]	
5	”	”
	GOLD.	
	MADRAS OLD STAR PAGODA.	
6	Figure of Vishnu with a star above the head.	Granulated surface with a 5-rayed star. [Pl. xi, 3.]
7	”	”
8	”	”
	BRASS.	
9	”	”

[1] Pagoda = 3½ rupees ; 1 rupee = 12 Fanams ; 14 paisa = 75 cash.

[2] This is the only copper coin of this type which I have ever seen or heard of, and was obtained from Mr. Desika Chari. *Auct.*

No.	Obverse.	Reverse.
	C. COINS WITHOUT DATE—*continued.*	
	MADRAS NEW DOUBLE STAR PAGODA.	
10	The gopuram of a temple surrounded by stars in centre: inscription round margin TWO PAGODAS. دو هون [1]	Figure of Vishnu surrounded with dots in centre: inscription round margin "Two Pagodas" in Tamil and Telugu.
	(OBLIQUE MILLING.)	[Pl. xi, 4.]
11	"	"
	MADRAS NEW SINGLE STAR PAGODA.	
12	" but inscription PAGODA هون [2]	" but inscription "Pagoda" in Tamil and Telugu. [Pl. xi, 5.]
	(OBLIQUE MILLING).	
	MADRAS SINGLE MOHUR.	
13	Arms of the Company and inscription ENGLISH EAST INDIA COMPANY: dotted rim on face.	کمپنی انگریز بہادر اشرفی ("Ashrafi of the Honorable English Company:") dotted rim on face.
	(STRAIGHT MILLING.)	[Pl. xi, 6.]
14	"	"
	MADRAS ½ MOHUR.	
15	Lion l. holding crown, and inscription ENGLISH EAST INDIA COMPANY: dotted rim on face.	کمپنی انگریز بہادر نیم اشرفی ("Half ashrafi of the Honorable English Company:") dotted rim on face.
	(STRAIGHT MILLING.)	[Pl. xi, 7.]
	MADRAS ¼ MOHUR.	
16	"	کمپنی انگریز بہادر پاو اشرفی ("Quarter ashrafi of the Honorable English Company:") dotted rim on face.

[1] "Two hún."

[2] "Hún."

No.	Obverse.	Reverse.
	C. COINS WITHOUT DATE—*continued.*	
	(STRAIGHT MILLING.)	
		[Pl. xi, 8.]
	MADRAS 5 RUPEES.	
17	Shield with lion l holding crown, and inscription ENGLISH EAST INDIA COMPÁNY: dotted rim on face.	پنجروپیه کمپنی انگریز بهادر ("Five Rupees of the Honorable English Company:") dotted rim on face.
	(STRAIGHT MILLING.)	
		[Pl. xi, 9.]
18	,,	,,
19	,,	,,
	BOMBAY GOLD RUPEE.	
20	.... بادشاه غازی	.... سنه جلوس ....
		[Pl. xi, 10.]
	SILVER.	
	MADRAS ? CHARLES II.	
21	Figure of Vishnu.	Two linked C's.
		[Pl. xi, 12.]
22	,,	,,
23	,,	,,
24	,,	,,
		[Pl. xi, 12.]
25	,,	,,
26	,, but surrounded by beaded circle.	,, but surrounded by beaded circle.
		[Pl. xv, 8.]
27	,,	,,

No.	Obverse.	Reverse.
	C. COINS WITHOUT DATE—*continued.*	
	COPPER.	
	BOMBAY DOUBLE PICE.	
28	A crown.	Motto [AU] SPICIO [REG] IS ET [SENATUS] ANG [LIAE. [Pl. xv, 9.]
29	"	"
	BOMBAY PICE.	
30	"	" [Pl. xv, 10.]
31	"	
	BOMBAY ?	
32	A crown with wreath below.	Undecipherable Persian inscription. [Pl. xvi, 7.]
	LEAD.	
	BOMBAY DOUBLE PICE.	
33	A crown with G.R. above, BOMB below.	Motto AUSPICIO REGIS ET SENATUS ANGLIÆ. [Pl. xvi, 8.]
	COPPER.	
	MADRAS.	
34	Orb and cross inscribed C.C. E. within a beaded circle.	Undecipherable inscription within a beaded circle. [Pl. xv, 11.]
	BOMBAY PICE.	
35	Bale-mark of the Company.	1 PICE BOMB. [Pl. xi, 13.]
	MADRAS.	
36	"*Sri.*" (Tamil).	"Kumpaní" (Tamil). [Pl. xii, 1.]
37	"	"

No.	Obverse.	Reverse.
	C. COINS WITHOUT DATE—*continued.*	
	COPPER—*continued.*	
38	Bale-mark of the Company: surrounded by a beaded circle.	Crossed lines and symbols. [Pl. xii, 2.]
39	"	"
40	"	"
41	"	"
42	"	Persian inscription. [Pl. xii, 3.]
43	Bale-mark of the Company.	Bale-mark of the Company.
	MADRAS 40 CASH.	
44	این چهل کاس است ("This is Forty Cash") XL CASH: serrated rim on face.	Inscription in Tamil and Telugu, "This is Forty Cash:" serrated rim on face. [Pl. xii, 4.]
45	"	"
	MADRAS 20 CASH.	
46	این بیست کاس است ("This is Twenty Cash") XX CASH.	Inscription in Tamil and Telugu, "This is Twenty Cash." [Pl. xii, 5.]
	MADRAS 10 CASH.	
47	این ده کاس است ("This is Ten Cash.") X CASH.	Inscription in Tamil and Telugu, "This is Ten Cash." [Pl. xii, 6.]

No.	Obverse.	Reverse.
	C. COINS WITHOUT DATE—*continued.*	
	COPPER—*continued.*	
	MADRAS 10 CASH—*continued.*	
48	این ده کاس اسی ("This is Ten Cash") X CASH.	Inscription in Tamil and Telugu "This is Ten Cash."
49	,,	,,
	MADRAS 5 CASH.	
50	این پنچ کاس اسی ("This is Five Cash") V CASH.	Inscription in Tamil and Telugu "This is Five Cash." [Pl. xii. 7.]
51	,,	,,
	MADRAS 2½ CASH.	
52	این دو و نیم کاس اسی ("This is Two-and-a-half Cash") 2½ CASH: surrounded by a circle of dots.	Inscription in Tamil and Telugu "This is Two-and-a-half Cash:" surrounded by a circle of dots. [Pl. xii, 8.]
53	,,	,,
	MADRAS ¼ DUB.	
54	Inscription in Tamil "Quarter Dub of the Company."	Inscription in Telugu "Quarter Dub of the Company." [Pl. xiii, 6.]
	BENGAL TWO PA'Í SIKKA.	
55	سنہ جلوس ۳۷ شاہ عالم بادشاہ ("In the 37th year of the reign of the Emperor Sháh alam.")	Inscription in Bengálí, Persian, and Nágarí "Two Pá'í Sikka." [Pl. xii, 10.]
	BENGAL ONE PA'Í SIKKA.	
56	,,	Inscription in Bengálí, Persian, and Nágarí "One Pa'í Sikka." [Pl. xiii, 1.]
57	,,	,,
58	,, but plain rim on face.	,, but plain rim on face. [Pl. xiii, 2.]

C. COINS WITHOUT DATE—*continued.*

COPPER—*continued.*

No.	Obverse.	Reverse.
59	سنه جلوس ٣٧ شاه عالم بادشاه ("In the 37th year of the reign of the Emperor Sháh Alam:") but plain rim on face.	Inscription in Bengalí, Persian, and Nágarí "One Pa'í Sikka:" but plain rim on face.
60	,, but lined circle on face.	Inscription in Persian and Nágarí "One Pa'í Sikka:" lined circle on face. [Pl. xiii, 3.]

BENGAL ½ PA'Í SIKKA.

No.	Obverse.	Reverse.
61	,,	Inscription in Persian and Nágarí "Half Pa'í Sikka:" lined circle on face. [Pl. xiii, 4.]

BENGAL ½ ANNA.

No.	Obverse.	Reverse.
62	Inscription in English and Bengálí "Half Anna:" serrated rim on face.	Inscription in Persian and Nágarí "Half Anna:" serrated rim on face. [Pl. xiii, 5.]

BENGAL 1 PIE.[1]

No.	Obverse.	Reverse.
63	Inscription in English and Bengálí, "One Pie:" serrated rim on face.	Inscription in Persian and Nagárí "One Pie:" serrated rim on face. [Pl. xii, 9.]
64	,,	,,

SILVER.

MADRAS 4 ANNAS.

No.	Obverse.	Reverse.
65	Centre, چهار آنه روپیه;[2] around, FOUR ANNAS.	Centre, "Four Annas" (Telugu): around, "Four Annas" (Tamil) and a star.

(OBLIQUE MILLING.)

No.	Obverse.	Reverse.
66	,,	,, [Pl. xiii, 7.]

[1] "The pá'í or third of a paisá has . . . . . . merely the name "one pá'í, which makes it liable to be confounded with the "one pá'í sikká," and on this account, perhaps, it has not found ready currency. The natives reckon only sixty-four paisá to the rupee, while the English accounts divide the áná into twelve pá'í; to distinguish them, this latter (hitherto an imaginary coin) was called the pá'í of account." Prinsep.

[2] "Four annas *rupia.*"

C. COINS WITHOUT DATE—*continued.*

SILVER—*continued.*

MADRAS 2 ANNAS.

No.	Obverse.	Reverse.
67	Centre, دو آنه روپيه [1]; around, TWO ANNAS.	Centre, "Two Annas" (Telugu) around, "Two Annas" (Tamil) and a star.

(OBLIQUE MILLING.)

[Pl. xiii, 8.]

No.	Obverse.	Reverse.
68	,,	,,

MADRAS ½ PAGODA.

No.	Obverse.	Reverse.
69	The gopuram of a temple surrounded by stars in centre: inscription round margin HALF PAGODA نيم هون پهولی.[2]	Figure of Vishnu surrounded by dots in centre: inscription round margin "Half Star Pagoda" in Tamil and Telugu.

(OBLIQUE MILLING.)

[Pl. xiv, 1.]

No.	Obverse.	Reverse.
70	,,	,,

MADRAS ¼ PAGODA.

No.	Obverse.	Reverse.
71	,, but inscription QUARTER PAGODA چهار هون پهولی[3].	,, but inscription "Quarter Star Pagoda" in Tamil and Telugu.

(OBLIQUE MILLING.)

[Pl. xiv, 2.]

No.	Obverse.	Reverse.
72	,,	,,

MADRAS 5 FANAMS.

No.	Obverse.	Reverse.
73	Centre, پانچ فلم; [4]; around, FIVE FANAMS.	Centre, "Five Rukalu" (Telugu); around, "Five Panams" (Tamil) and a star.

(OBLIQUE MILLING.)

[Pl. xiv, 3.]

[1] "Two annas *rupia.*"
[2] "Half *puli* hun."
[3] "Quarter *puli* hun."
[4] "Five falams."

C. COINS WITHOUT DATE—*continued.*

SILVER—*continued.*

No.	Obverse.	Reverse.
74	Centre, فلم پنج ; around, FIVE FANAMS.	Centre, "Five Rukalu" (Telugu); around, "Five Panams" (Tamil) and a star.
75	,,	,,
76	,,	,, but no star.

(THICK COIN.)

[Pl. xvi, 9.]

MADRAS DOUBLE FANAM.

No.	Obverse.	Reverse.
77	Centre, دو فلم [1]; around, DOUBLE FANAM.	Centre, "Two Rukalu" (Telugu); around, "Two Panams" (Tamil) and a star.

(OBLIQUE MILLING.)

[Pl. xiv, 4.]

No.	Obverse.	Reverse.
78	,,	,,
79	,,	,,

MADRAS FANAM.

No.	Obverse.	Reverse.
80	Centre, فلم [2]; around, FANAM.	Centre, "Ruka" (Telugu); around, "Panam" (Tamil) and a star.

(OBLIQUE MILLING.)

[Pl. xiv, 5.]

No.	Obverse.	Reverse.
81	,,	,,
82	A star in centre: surrounded by the word FANAM and a wreath.	A star in centre: surrounded by the words "Ruka" (Telugu) and "Panam" (Tamil). [Pl. xiv, 6.]
83	,,	,,

[1] "Two falams."

[2] "One falam."

ADDENDA.

During the revision of the later proof sheets, I had the opportunity of examining a large number of coins from the Ganjam district, out of which the following coins of the Company have been added :—

P. 93. Nos. 145·1 and 145·2. Gold Mohur. (Lion and Palm Tree). 1841.

P. 96. No. 4·1. Murshidábád rupee, oblique milling.

„ „ Nos. 4·3 and 4·2. Murshidábád $\frac{1}{2}$ rupee, oblique milling.

„ „ Nos. 4·4 and 4·5· Murshidábád $\frac{1}{4}$ rupee, oblique milling.

P. 97. No. 7·1. Murshidábád $\frac{1}{2}$ rupee, straight milling.

„ „ No. 8·1. Murshidábád $\frac{1}{4}$ rupee, straight milling.

P. 98. No. 12·1. Murshidábád $\frac{1}{4}$ rupee, without milling.

„ „ No. 13·1. Farukhábád $\frac{1}{2}$ rupee, oblique milling.

P. 102. Nos. 41·1 and 41·2. Thick Surat rupee, without date incuse.

„ „ Nos. 42·1—42 7. Old sun 19 sikka rupees, and $\frac{1}{4}$ rupees.

P. 106. Nos. 65·1—65·31. Arcot rupees of the same type as No. 65, with various dates.

„ „ Nos. 67·1—67·3. Arcot $\frac{1}{2}$ and $\frac{1}{4}$ rupees of the same type as No. 67.

INDEX TO PLATES.

PLATE I.

Fig.	Metal.	Date.	Description of Coin.	Page.
1	Ae.	1722	Madras.	79
2	,,	1733	,,	28, 79
3	,,	,,	,,	79
4	,,	1736	,,	28, 79
5	,,	1737	,,	79
6	,,	1755	,,	28, 79
7	,,	1756	,,	28, 79
8	,,	1786	,,	28, 80
9	,,	1791	Bombay. 10 Cash.	80
10	,,	1794	,, 20 ,,	81
11	,,	١٢١٢	Madras. Cash.	83
12	,,	1801	Madras.	83
13	,,	180x	,,	83

PLATE II.

Fig.	Metal.	Date.	Description of Coin.	Page.
1	Ar.	1799 ?	Tellicherry.	21, 83
2	,,	,,	,,	21, 83
3	Ae.	1801	Madras. 2 Dubs.	83
4	,,	,,	,, ½ Dub.	83
5	,,	,,	,, ,, ,,	83
6	,,	1803	,, 1 Cash.	84
7	,,	,,	,, ,, ,,	84
8	,,	,,	,, ,, ,,	84
9	,,	,,	,, 10 ,,	85
10	,,	,,	,, 5 ,,	85
11	,,	1804	Bombay. 10 ,,	85

PLATE III.

Fig.	Metal.	Date.	Description of Coin.	Page.
1	Ae.	1804	Bombay. 5 Cash.	89
2	Ar.	1805	Tellicherry.	21, 86
3	,,	,,	,,	21, 86
4	Au.	180*x*	,,	22, 86
5	Ae.	1807	Madras.	86
6	,,	1808	Madras. 20 Cash.	87
7	,,	1807	,, 3 Dubs.	87
8	,,	1816	Bombay. 4 Pice.	88
9	,,	,,	,, 2 ,,	88
10	,,	,,	,, Single.	88

PLATE IV.

Fig.	Metal.	Date.	Description of Coin.	Page.
1	Ae.	1821	Bombay. ½ Pice.	89
2	,,	1825	,, Single Pice.	89
3	,,	1825	,, ½ ,,	89
4	,,	18*xx*	,, Single ,,	89
5	,,	1825	,, 4 Paí.	90
6	,,	,,	,, 2 ,,	90
7	,,	,,	,, 1 ,,	90
8	,,	1833	,, ¼ Anna.	90
9	,,	,,	,, 1 Pie.	90
10	,,	1834	,, ½ Anna.	90

PLATE V.

Fig.	Metal.	Date.	Description of Coin.	Page.
1	Au.	1835	Double Mohur.	91
2	,,	,,	Single ,,	91
3	Ar.	,,	1 Rupee.	91
4	,,	,,	½ ,,	91
5	,,	,,	¼ ,,	92
6	Ae.	,,	½ Anna.	92
7	,,	,,	¼ ,,	92
8	,,	,,	$\frac{1}{12}$,,	92
9	Ar.	1841	2 Annas.	94

PLATE VI.

Fig.	Metal.	Date.	Description of Coin.	Page.
1	Au.	١٢٠٢	Murshidábád. Mohur.	96
2	,,	١٢٠٣	,, ¼ ,,	96
3	Ar.	*Sun*. 19	,, Rupee.	97
4	,,	,,	,, ½ ,,	97
5	,,	١٢٠٣	,, ¼ ,,	97
6	,,	*Sun*. 19	,, Rupee.	97
7	,,	,,	,, ½ ,,	98
8	,,	١٢٠٣	,, ¼ ,,	98

PLATE VII.

Fig.	Metal.	Date.	Description of Coin.	Page.
1	Ar.	*Sun.* 45	Farukhábád Rupee.	98
2	,,	,,	,, ,,	98
3	,,	,,	,, ,,	99
4	,,	,,	,, ½ ,,	99
5	,,	,,	,, ,, ,,	99
6	,,	١٢٠٣	,, ¼ ,,	99
7	,,	١٢٢٩	,, Rupee.	99
8	,,	,,	Benares. ¼ ,,	100

PLATE VIII.

Fig.	Metal.	Date.	Description of Coin.	Page.
1	Ar.	١٢٢٩	Benares. ½ Rupee.	100
2	,,	١٢١٥	Surat. Rupee.	101
3	,,	,,	,, ,,	101
4	,,	,,	,, ½ ,,	101
5	,,	,,	,, ¼ ,,	101

PLATE IX.

Fig.	Metal.	Date.	Description of Coin.	Page.
1	Ar.	١١٧٢	Arcot. Double Rupee.	102
2	,,	,,	,, Single ,,	103
3	,,	,,	,, 2 Annas.	103
4	,,	,,	,, 1 Anna	103
5	,,	,,	,, Rupee.	104
6	,,	,,	,, ½ ,,	104
7	,,	,,	,, ¼ ,,	104

PLATE X.

Fig.	Metal.	Date.	Description of Coin.	Page.
1	Au.	١١٧٢	Arcot. Mohur.	104
2	,,	,,	,, ½ ,,	105
3	Ar.	,,	,, Rupee.	105
4	,,	,,	,, ½ ,,	105
5	,,	,,	,, ¼ ,,	105
6	Au.	١٢١٣	,, Mohur.	106
7	Ar.	,,	,, Rupee.	106
8	,,	,,	,, ,,	106

PLATE XI.

Fig.	Metal.	Date.	Description of Coin.	Page.
1	Au.		Madras. 3 Swámi Pagoda	107
2	,,		,, Porto Novo ,,	13, 22, 107
3	,,		,, Old Star ,,	13, 14, 107
4	,,		,, New double Star ,,	14, 108
5	,,		,, Single ,, ,,	14, 108
6	,,		,, Mohur.	108
7	,,		,, ½ ,,	108
8	,,		,, ¼ ,,	109
9	,,		,, 5 Rupees.	109
10	,,		Bombay. Gold Rupee.	51, 109
11	Ar.		Madras ? Charles II.	20, 109
12	,,		,, ,, ,,	21, 109
13	Ae.	177x	Bombay. Pice.	80, 110

PLATE XII.

Fig.	Metal.	Date.	Description of Coin.	Page.
1	Ae.		Madras.	110
2	,,		,,	111
3			,,	111
4	,,		Madras. 40 Cash.	111
5	,,		,, 20 ,,	111
6	,,		,, 10 ,,	111
7	,,		,, 5 ,,	112
8	,,		,, 2½ ,,	112
9	,,		Bengal. 1 Pie.	113
10	,,		,, 2 Paí Sikka.	112

PLATE XIII.

Fig.	Metal.	Date.	Description of Coin.	Page.
1	Ae.		Bengal. 1 Pai Sikka.	112
2	,,		,, ,, ,,	112
3	,,		,, ,, ,,	113
4	,,		,, ½ ,, ,,	113
5	,,		,, ½ Anna.	113
6	,,		Madras. ½ Pie.	112
7	Ar.		,, 4 Annas.	113
8	,,		,, 2 ,,	114

PLATE XIV.

Fig.	Metal.	Date.	Description of Coin.	Page.
1	Ar.		Madras. ½ Pagoda.	114
2	,,		,, Single ,,	114
3	,,		,, 5 Fanams.	114
4	,,		,, Double Fanam.	115
5	,,		,, Single ,,	115
6	,,		,, ,, ,,	115

PLATE XV.

Fig.	Metal.	Date.	Description of Coin.	Page.
1	Ae.	1777	Bombay. Double Pice.	33, 79
2	,,	177*x*	,, ,, ,,	80
3	,,	1777	,, Single Pice.	33, 80
4	,,	1807	Madras. ½ Dub.	87
5	,,	1809	Bengal. Proof. 1 Pie.	88
6	,,	,,	,, ,, ½ ,,	88
7	,,	1821	Bombay. Pice.	89
8	Ar.		Madras? Charles II.	20, 109
9	Ae.		Bombay. Double Pice.	110
10	,,		,, Single ,,	110
11	,,		Madras.	110

PLATE XVI.

Fig.	Metal.	Date.	Description of Coin.	Page.
1	Ae.		Trisoolee. Pice.	100
2	,,		,, ,,	100
3	Au.		Surat. Mohur.	102
4	Ar.		,, Rupee.	102
5	,,	1825	,, ,,	102
6	,,	,,	,, ½ ,,	102
7	Ae.		Bombay. ?	110
8	Pb.		Bombay. Double Pice.	25, 29, 110
9	Ar.		Madras. 5 Fanams.	44, 115

PLATE XVII.

Fig.	Metal.	Date.	Description of Coin.	Page.
1	Ar.		Elizabeth. Crown.	7
2	,,		,, ½ ,,	7
3	,,		,, Shilling.	7
4	,,		,, Six pence.	8

PLATE XVIII.

Fig.	Metal.	Date.	Description of Coin.	Page.
1	Ar.	1667	Charles II. Rupee.	19
2	,,	1678	,, ,, ,,	19
3	Ae.		,, ,, Pice.	19
4	Ar.		,, ,, Rupee.	19
5	,,	1687	James II. ,,	21

PLATE XIX.

Fig.	Metal.	Date.	Description of Coin.	Page.
1	Ar.		George I. Madras. 3 Fanams.	26
2	,,		,, Double Fanam.	26
3	Ae.		,, Copper.	26
4	Pb.	1675?	Charles II. 2 Cash.	19
5	Ae.	1714	George I. Copper Coin.	26
6	,,		,, ,,	26
7	,,		,, ,,	26
8	,,	1728	George II. Double Pice.	28
9	,,		George III. ½ ,,	33
10	Pb.		,, ,, ¼ ,,	33
11	Ae.		?	
12	,,		?	

PLATE XX.

Fig.	Metal.	Date.	Description of Coin.	Page.
1	Ae.	173*x*	George II. Pice.	28
2	,,	1742	,, ,, ,,	28
3	,,	1813	George III. ¼ Pice.	33
4	Au.	1765	Bombay. Pattern Mohur.	35
5	,,	1770	,, ,, ,,	35
6	Ae.	1793	,, Proof. Copper.	38
7	Ar.	1834	Pattern. Rupee.	63
8	Ae.		Patna Post. One Anna.	63
9		1822	Benares. Pattern.	

Plate. I.

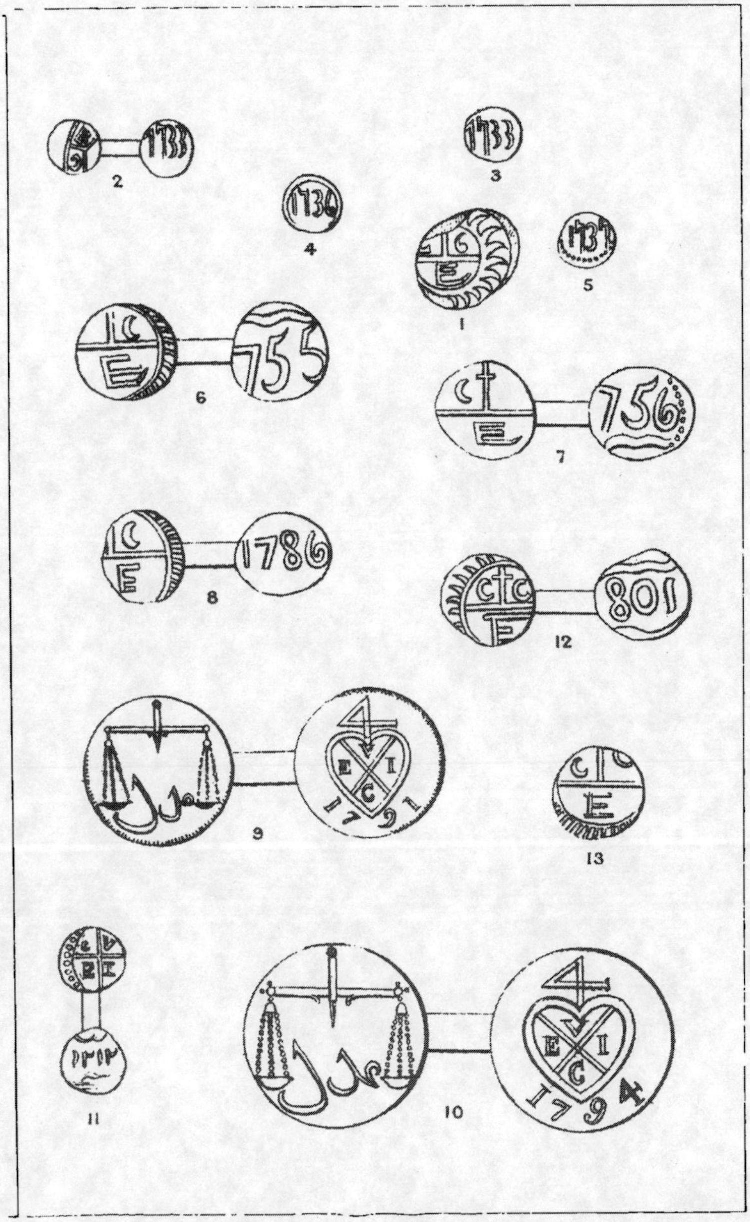

Plate II.

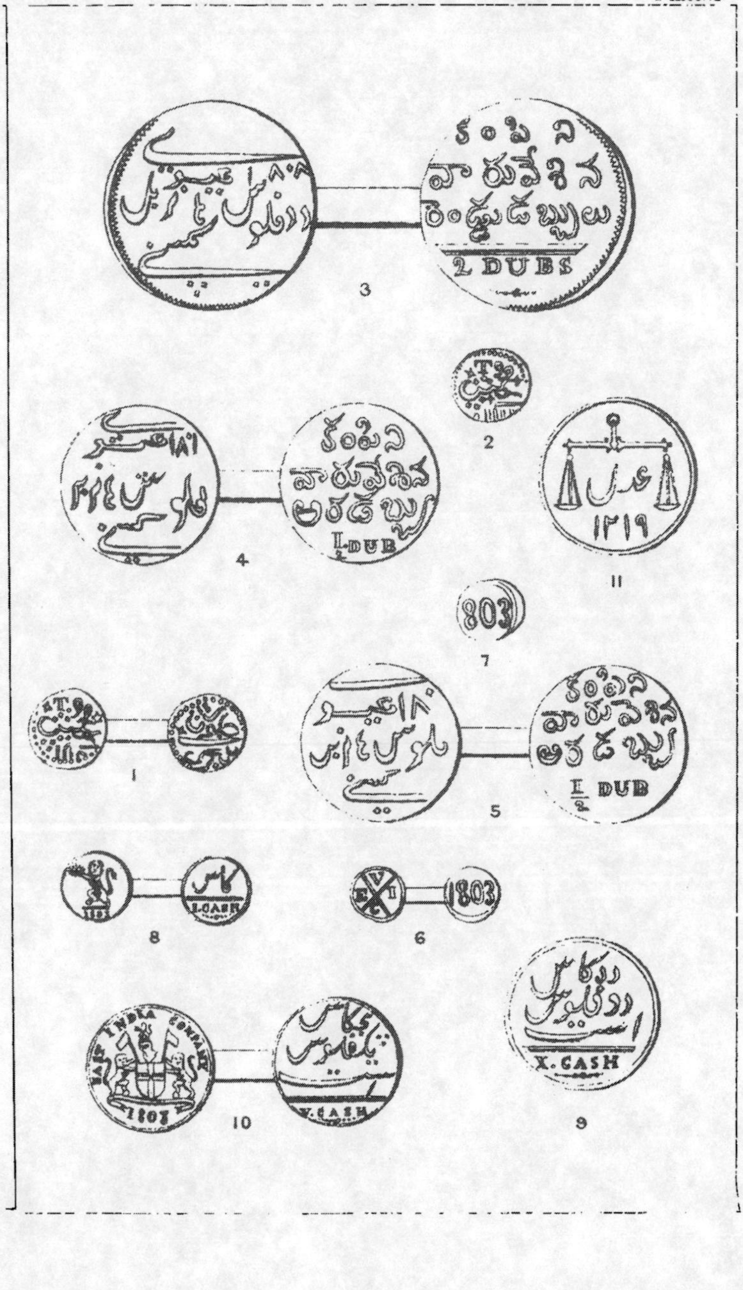
2 DUBS
3
2
½ DUB
4
1219
11
803
7
1
½ DUB
5
I. CASH
8
1803
6
X. CASH
9
EAST INDIA COMPANY
1803
V. CASH
10

Plate.III.

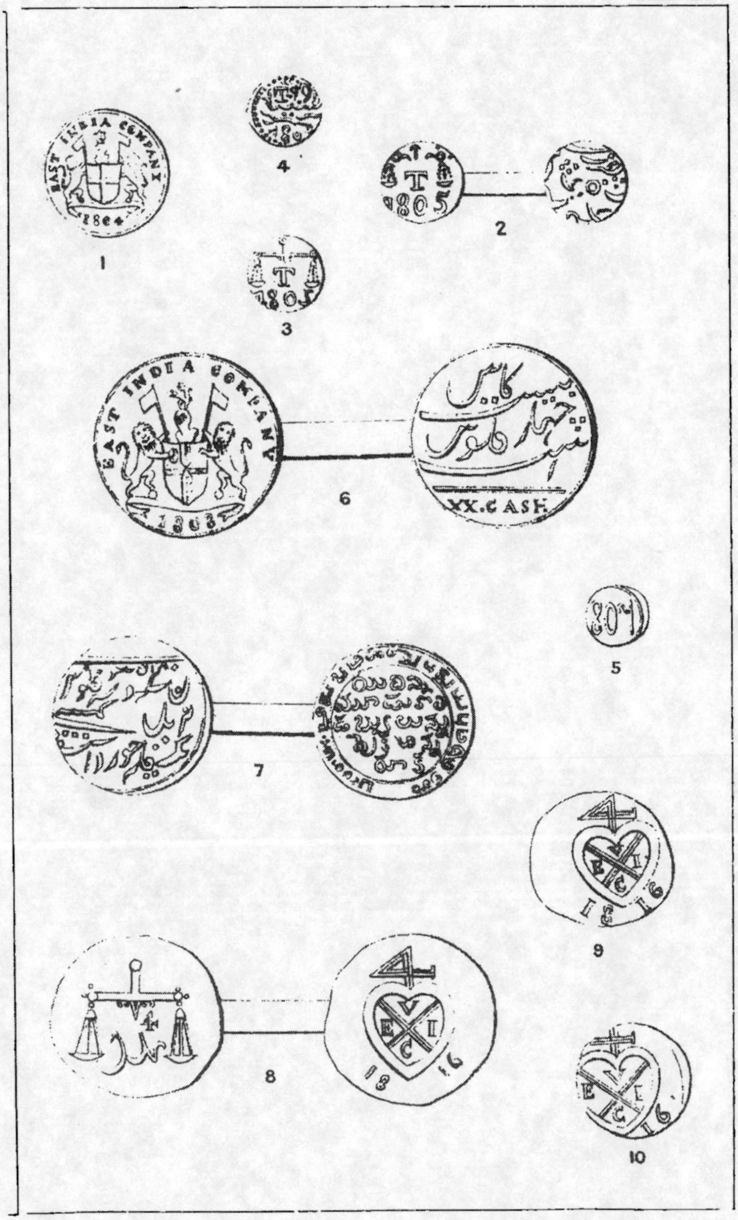

1
EAST INDIA COMPANY
1804
2
T
1805
3
T
1805
4
1808
5
1808
6
EAST INDIA COMPANY
1808
XX.CASH
7
8
4
V
E I
C
1816
9
4
E I
C
1816
10
V
E I
C
16

Plate. IV.

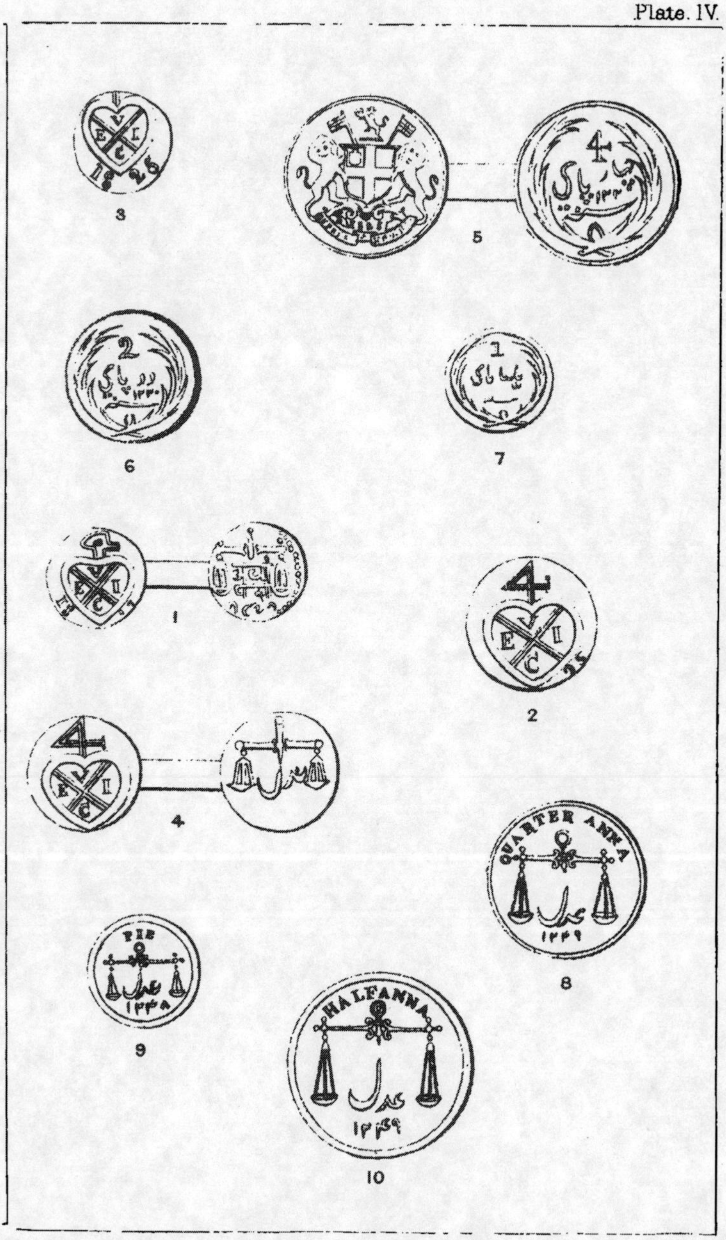

Plate. V.

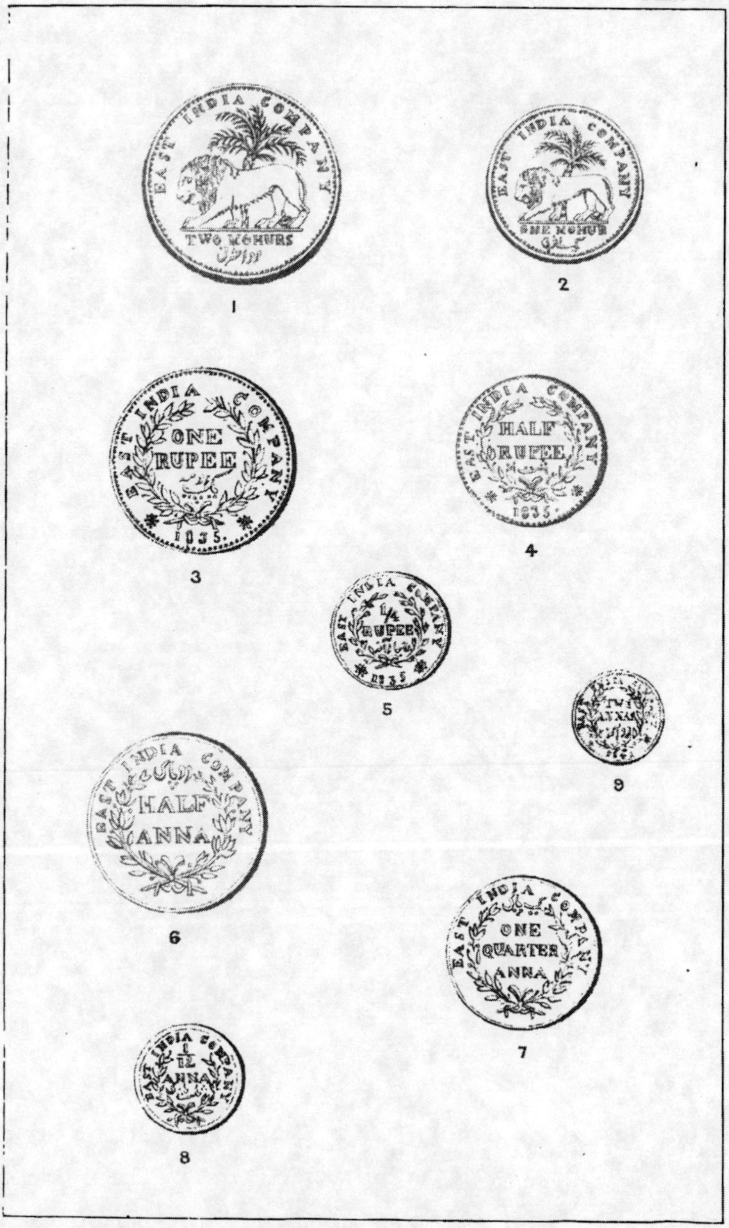

EAST INDIA COMPANY
TWO MOHURS
1
2
ONE
RUPEE
1835.
3
HALF
RUPEE
1835
4
1/4
RUPEE
1835
5
HALF
ANNA
6
ONE
QUARTER
ANNA
7
1/12
ANNA
8
9

Plate. VI.

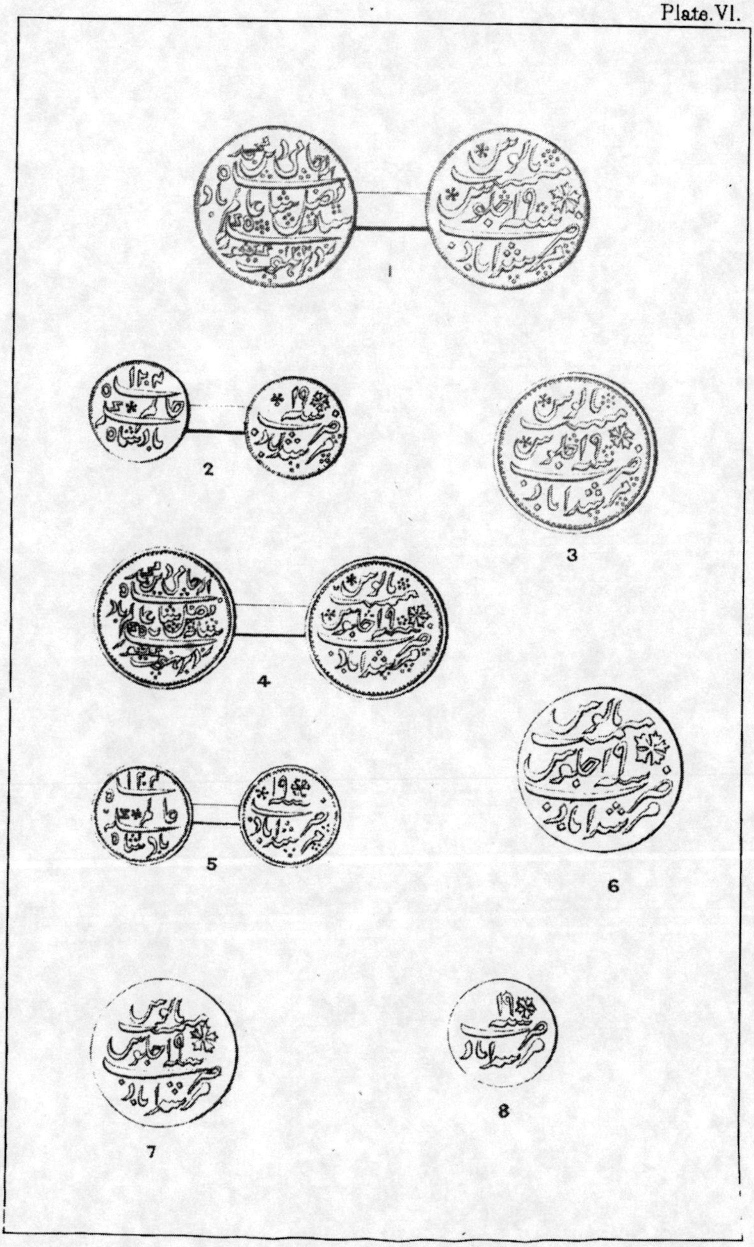

Plate.VII.

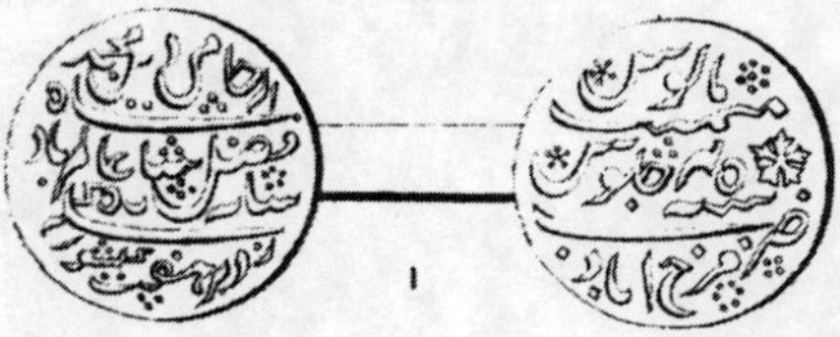

1

2

3

4

5

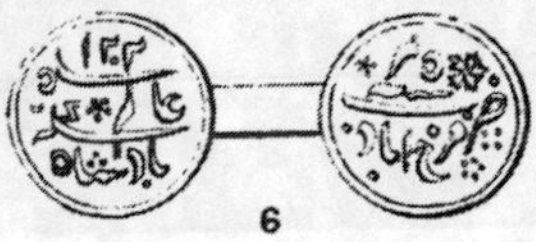

6

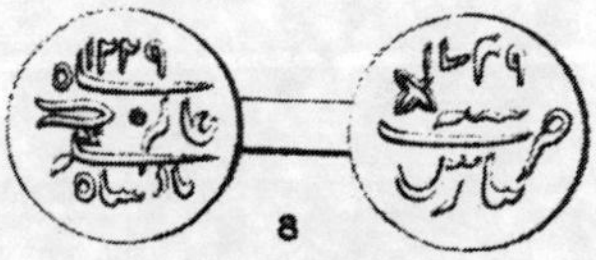

8

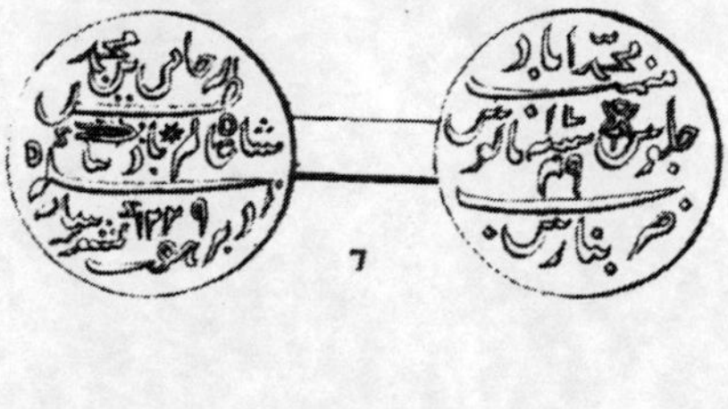

7

Plate. VIII.

1

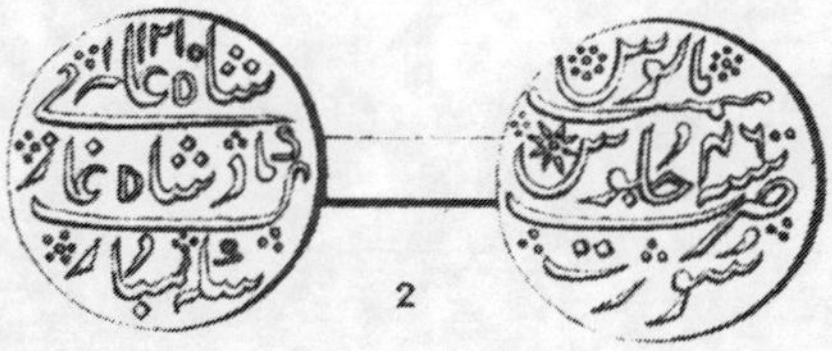

2

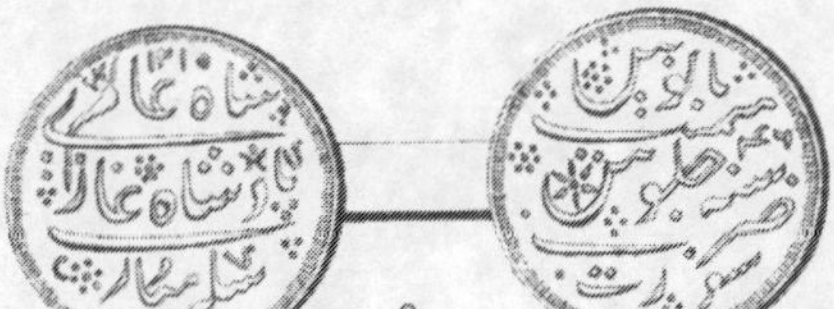

3

4

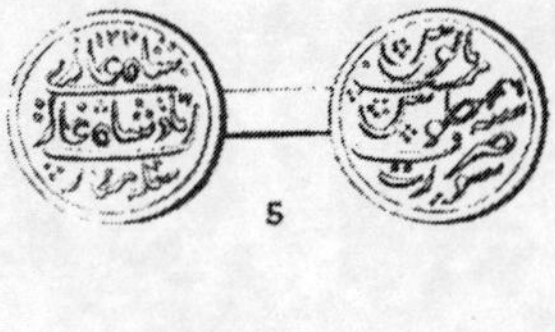

5

Plate IX.

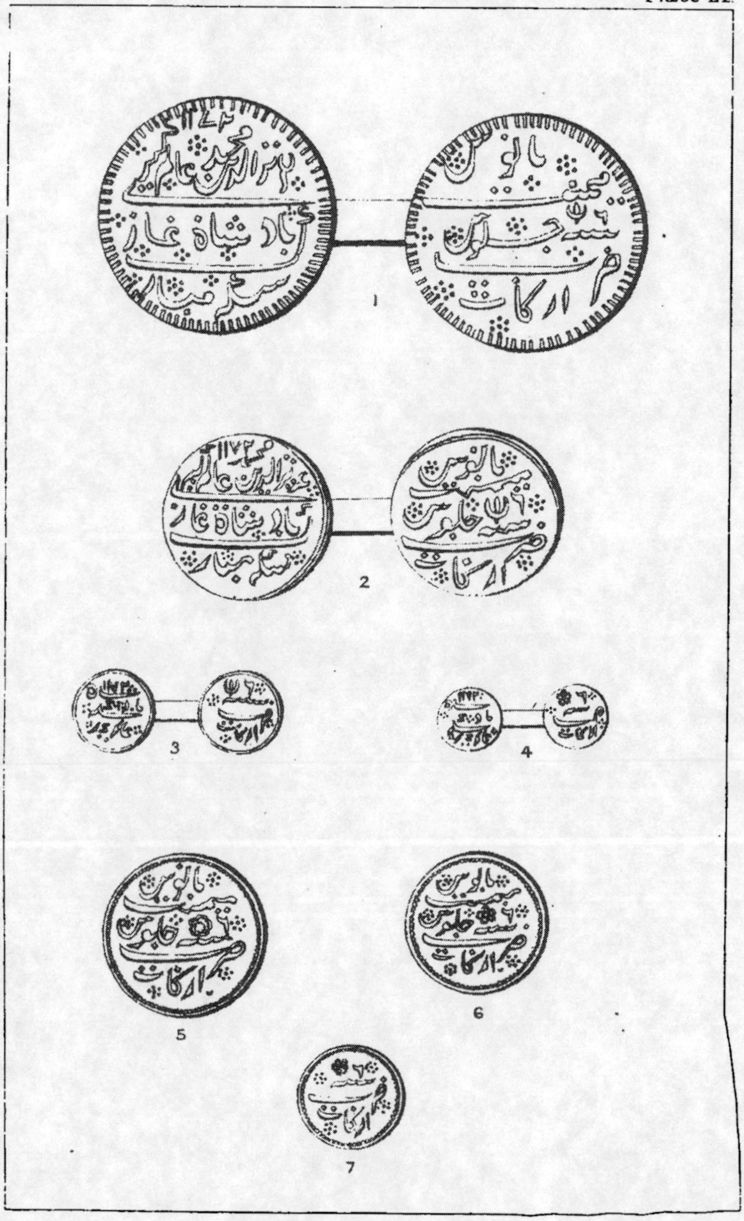

Plate X

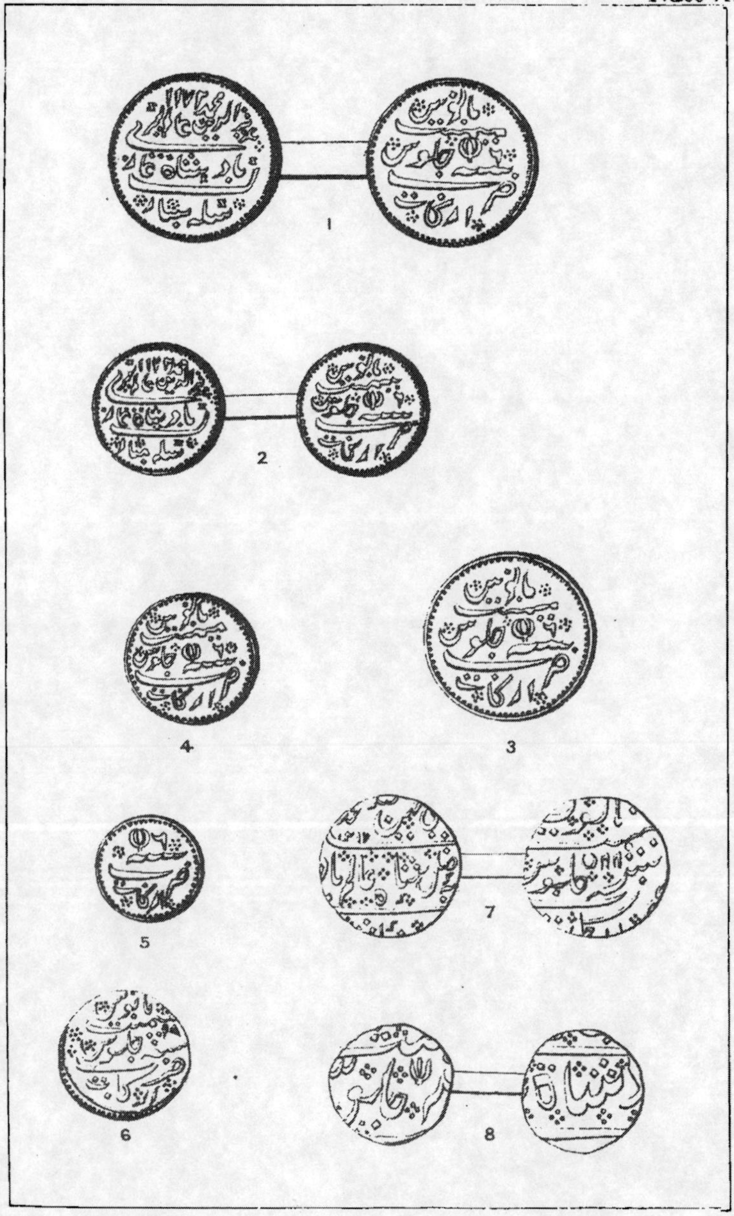

Plate XI.

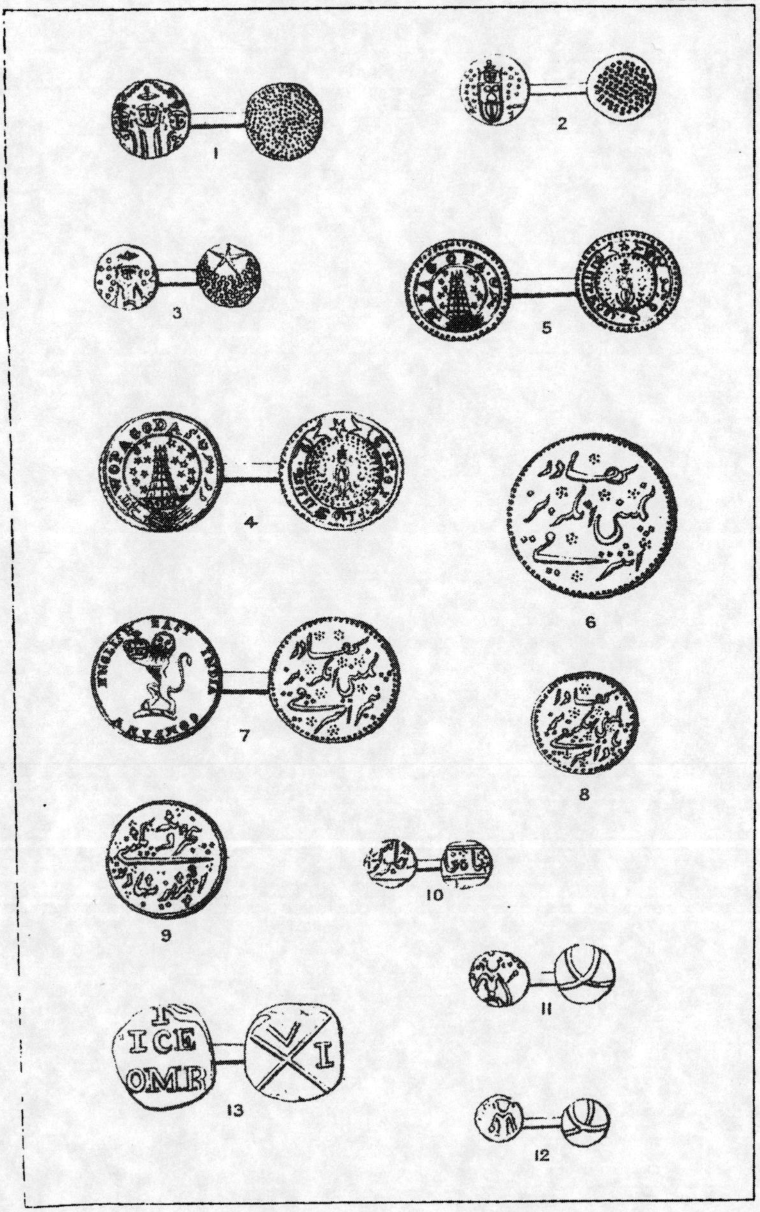

Plate XII.

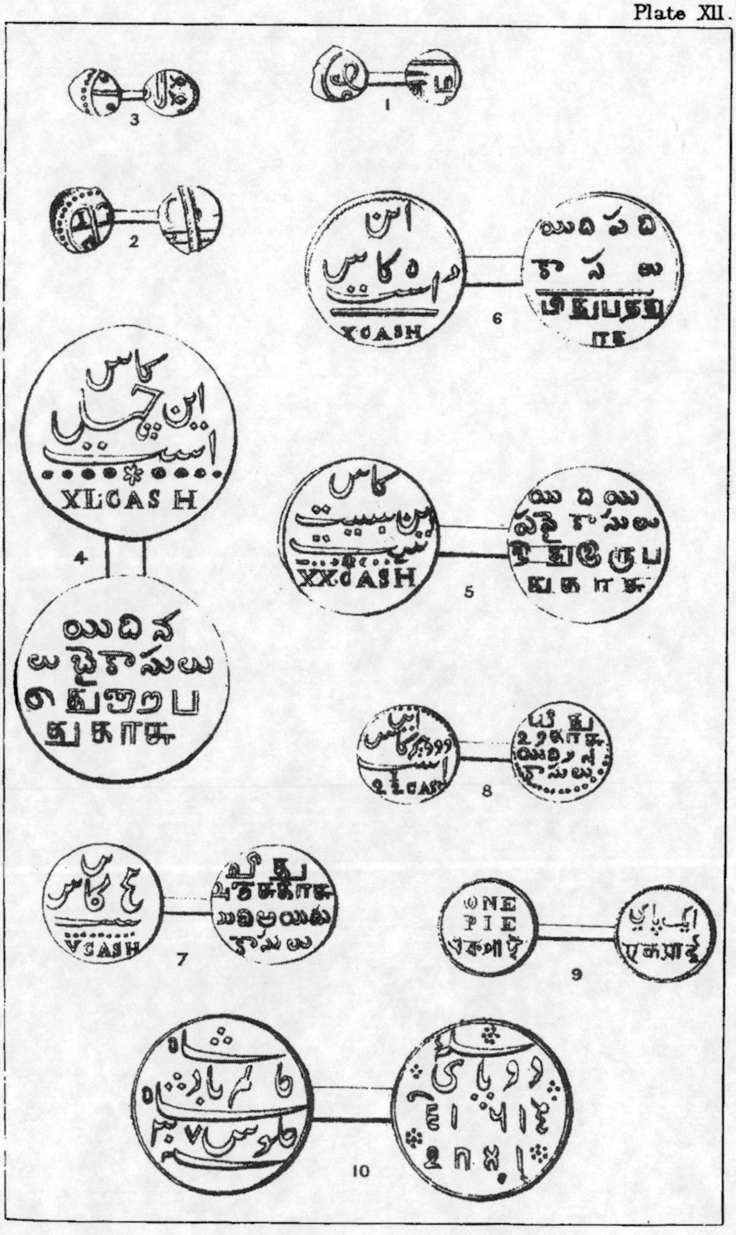

Plate XIII.

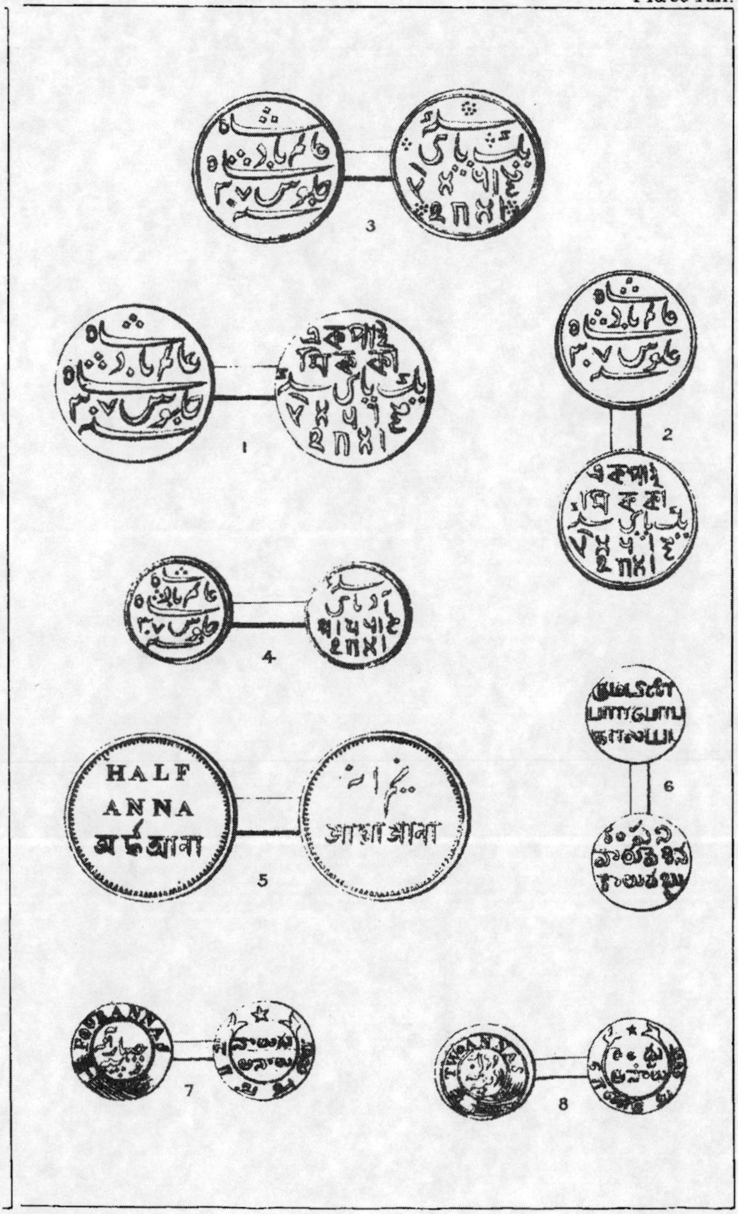

Plate XIV.

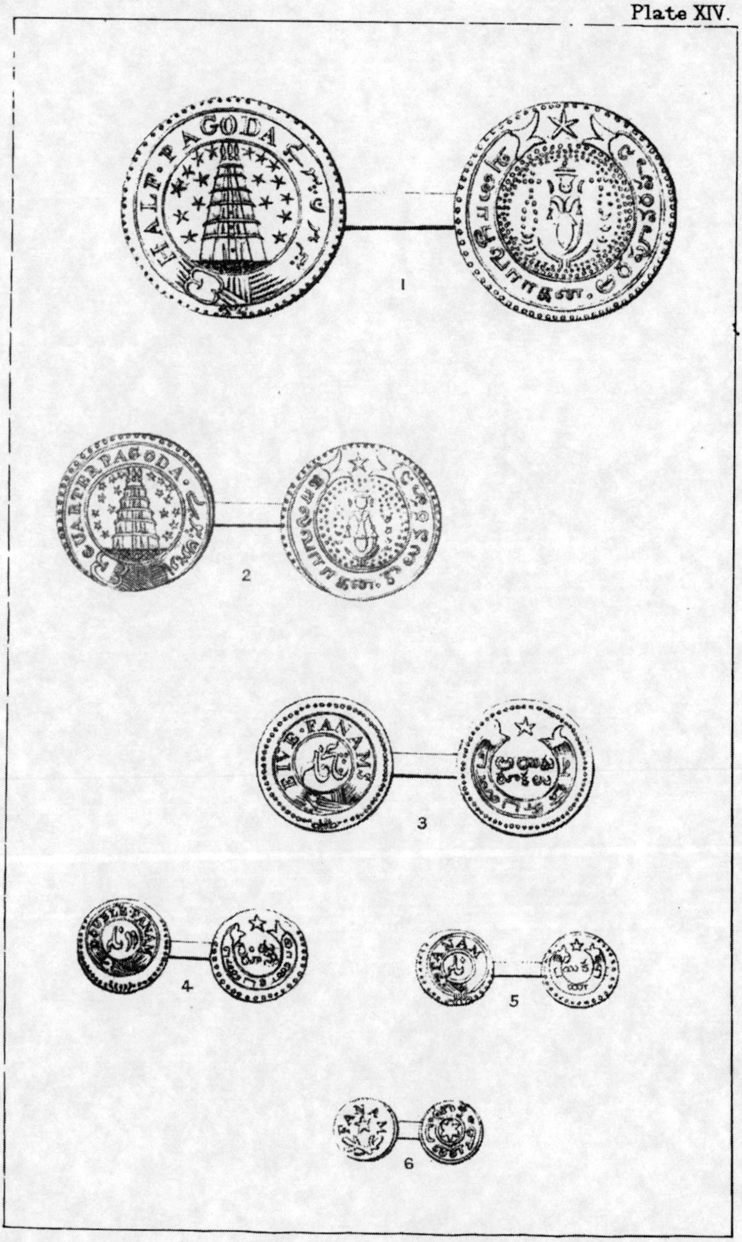
HALF·PAGODA
QUARTER PAGODA
FIVE·FANAMS
DOUBLE·FANAM
FANAM
FANAM

Plate XV.

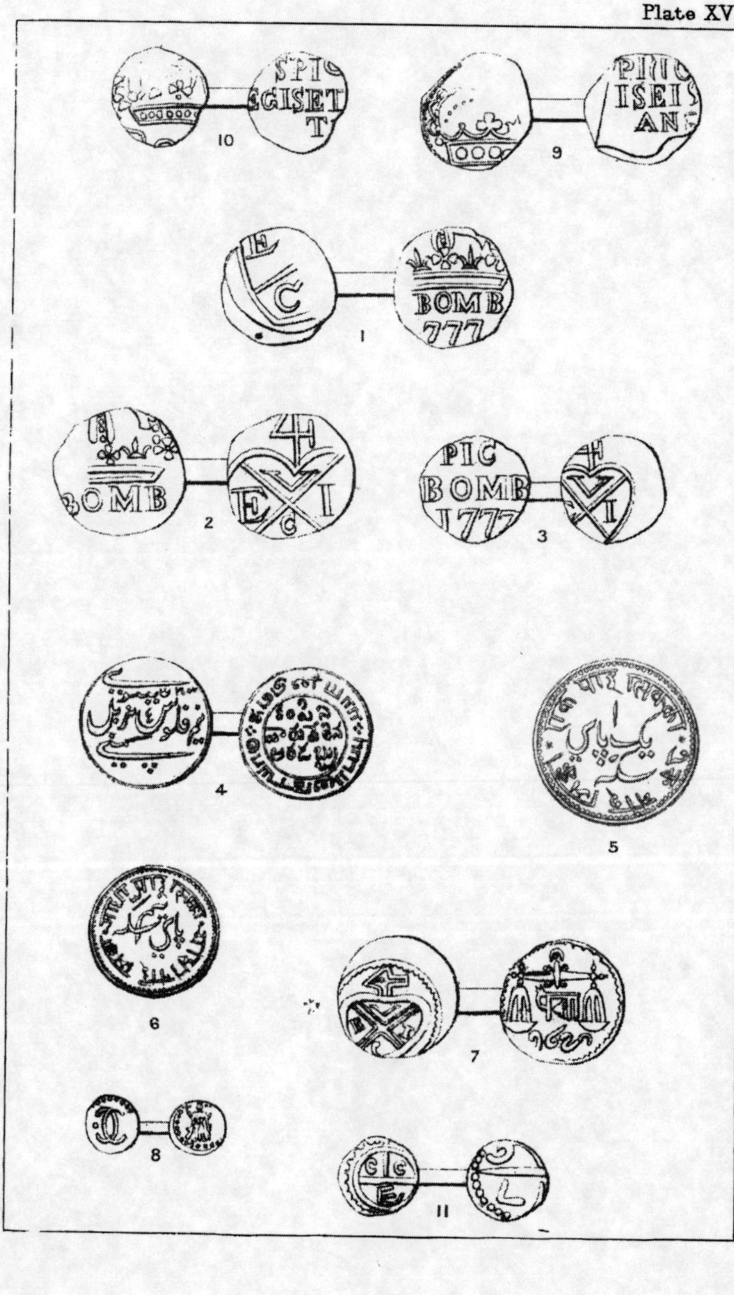

Plate XVI.

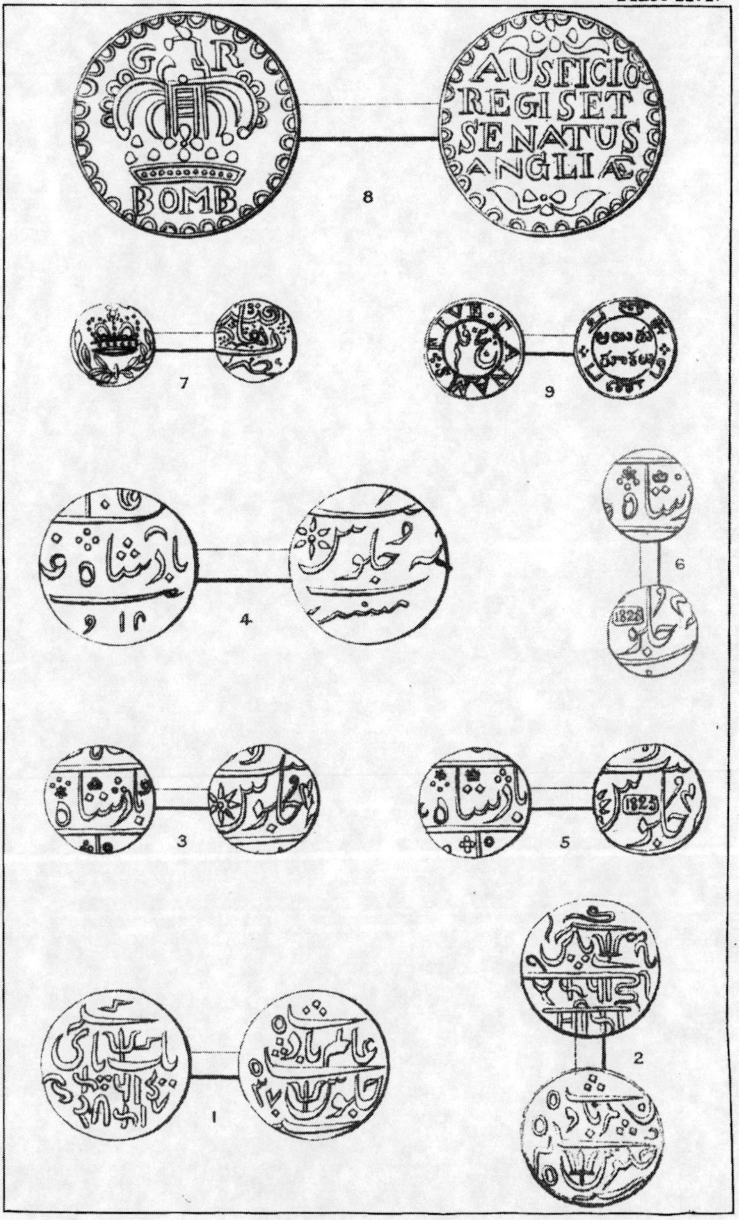

G R
BOMB
AUSPICIO REGIS ET SENATUS ANGLIÆ
8
7
9
4
6
1825
3
5
1823
1
2

Plate XVII.

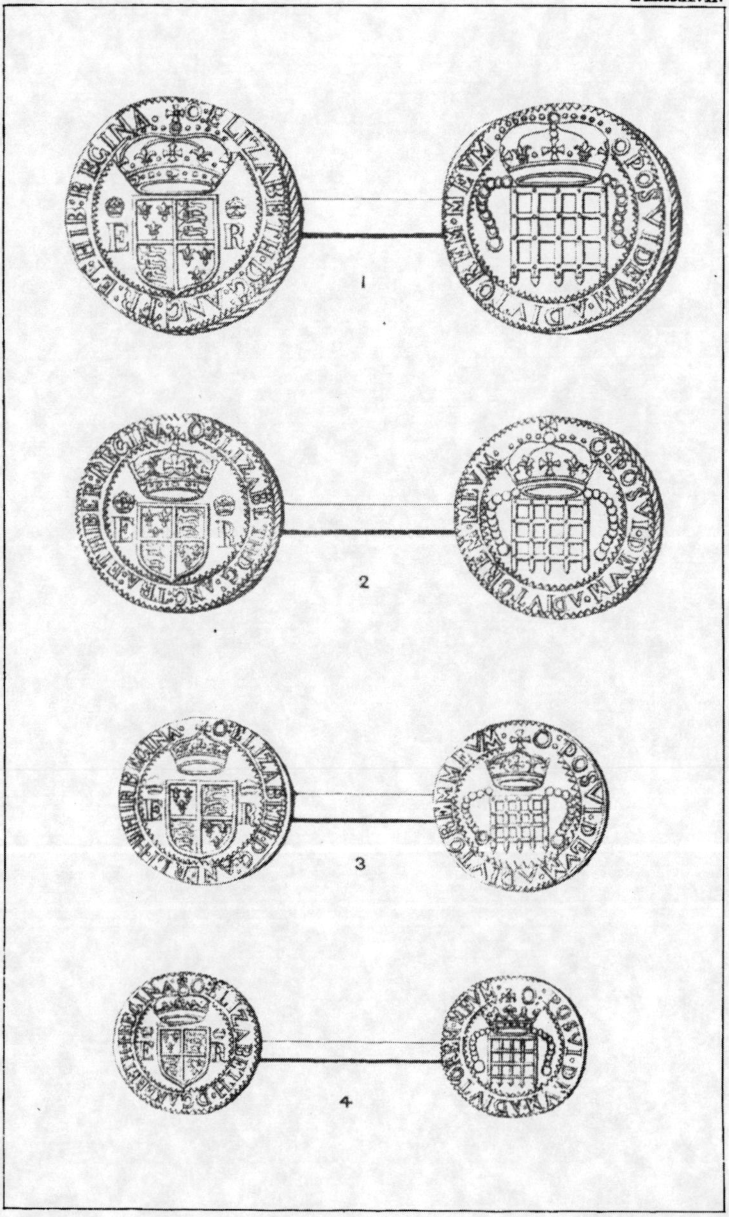
ELIZABETH D G ANG FR ET HIB REGINA
E R
POSVI DEVM ADIVTOREM MEVM
1
2
3
4

Plate XVIII.

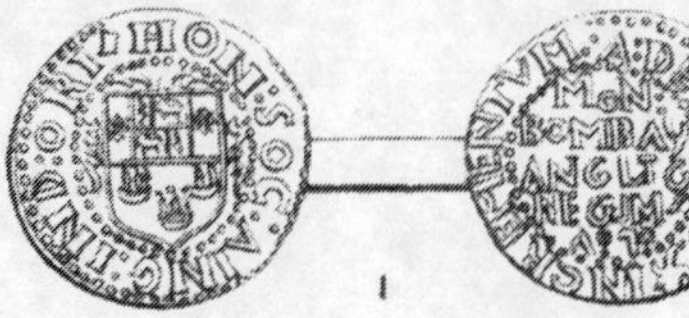

1

2

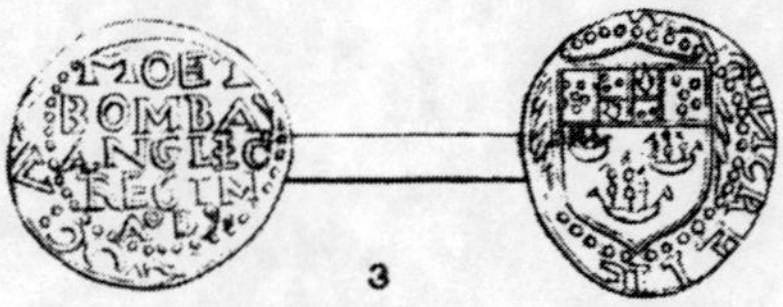

3

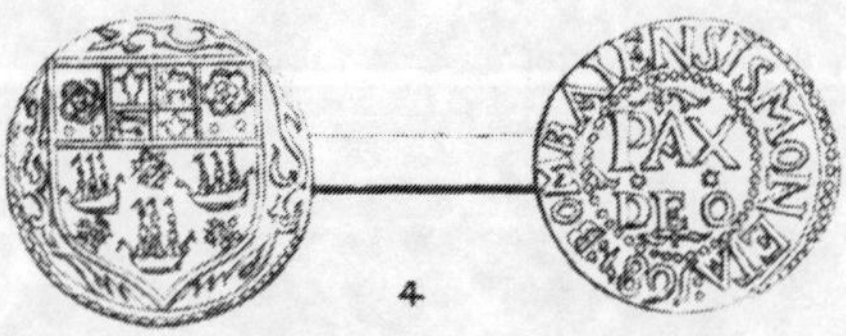

4

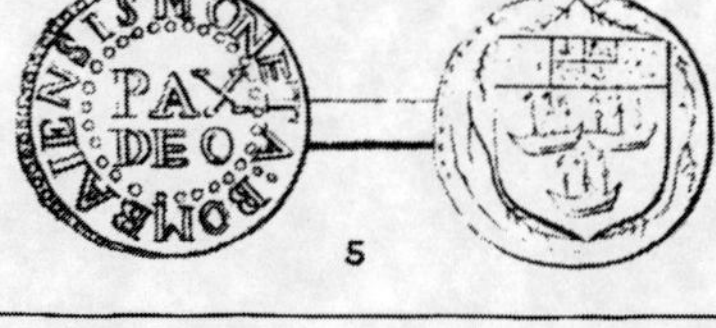

5

Plate XIX

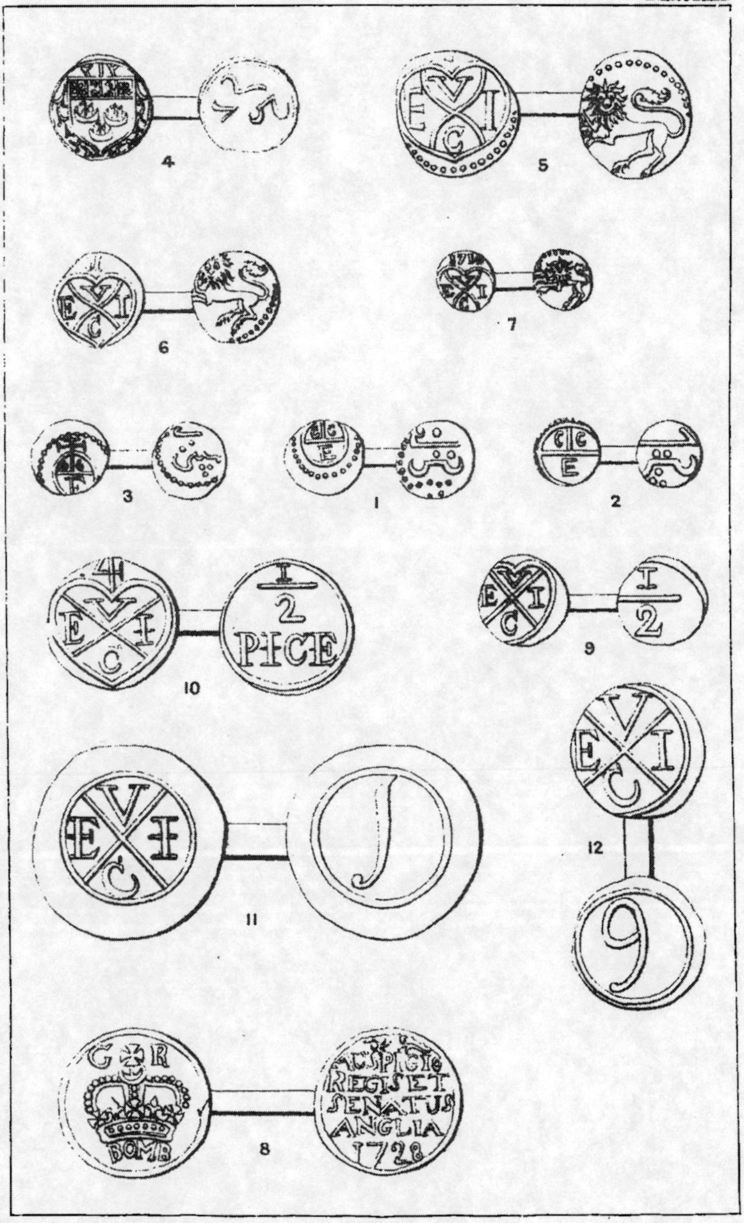

4
5
6
7
3
1
2
10
9
12
11
8
E V I C
2
PICE
9
G R
BOMB
REGIS ET
SENATUS
ANGLIA
1728

Plate XX.

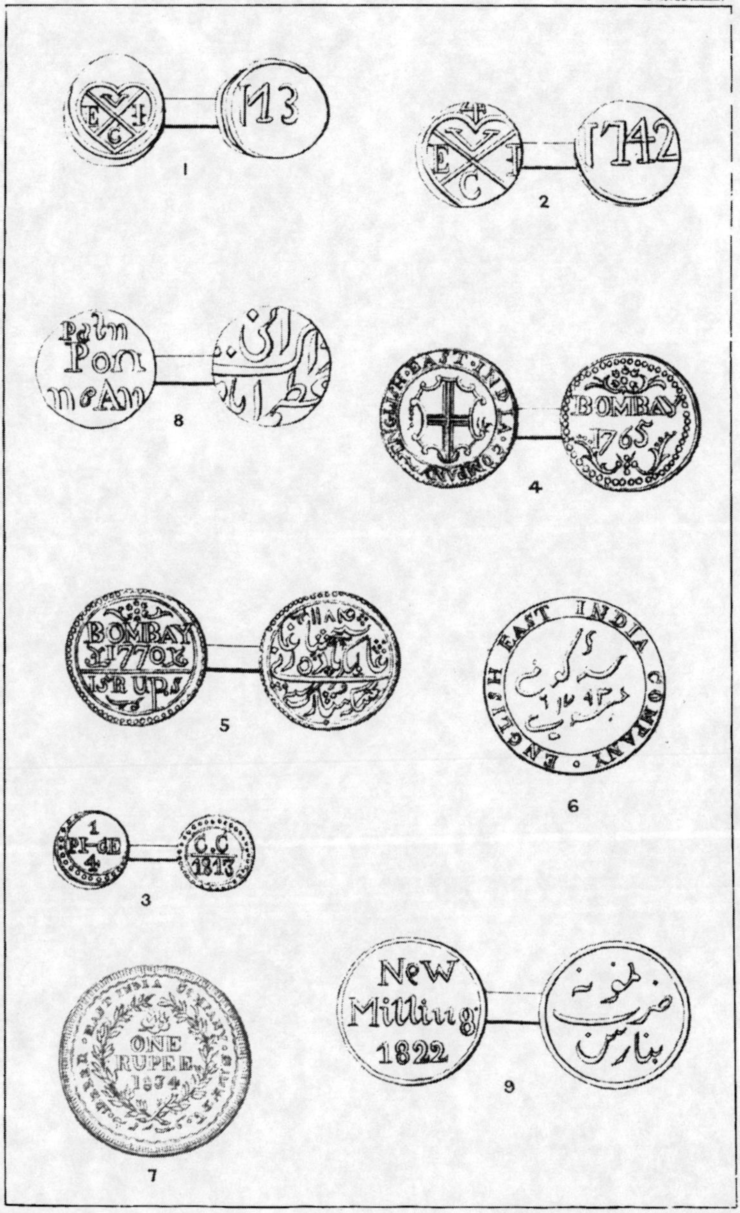

1
1742
2
BOMBAY
1765
4
8
BOMBAY
5
ENGLISH EAST INDIA COMPANY
6
C.C
1813
3
ONE
RUPEE
1834
7
New
Milling
1822
9